Human Drama

967
157

"In the drama of the bullring what a man sees is himself; his success or his failure to come to terms with his own life . . ."

With this challenging theme, Wright Morris, in his National Book Award novel, reveals the inner tumult of a group of touring Midwesterners as they sit transfixed by the spectacle of a bullfight in Mexico. As the pattern of life and death, honor and disgrace, unfolds before them in the sanded circle, their own lives jump into sharp focus. Ranging back in time, a middle-aged matron realizes how a kiss stolen long ago marred her marriage before it began. A flamboyant failure relives the childhood act of bravado which became the touchstone of his career. A complacent husband, an embittered pioneer, a lonely doctor—each is flooded with old memories and longings, faces his moment of truth, and emerges a changed being.

"Possibly not since Sinclair Lewis or Dreiser have the drabness and heart-yearnings of the plain, down-to-earth American in his search for limited happiness and security been delineated so surely."
—Wall Street Journal

"Mr. Morris has drawn a compelling modern fable out of familiar waywardness." *—New York Times*

"The image of American life that emerges from his whole work is unequalled by any author of his generation." *—The Reporter*

THIS IS A REPRINT OF THE HARDCOVER EDITION FIRST
PUBLISHED BY HARCOURT, BRACE, AND CO.

Other SIGNET Books You'll Enjoy Reading

A HIGH WIND IN JAMAICA (The Innocent Voyage)
by Richard Hughes

The bizarre classic about children captured by pirates; innocents overwhelmed by the evil inherent in them. Now a movie starring Anthony Quinn. (#P2648—60¢)

THE INJUSTICE COLLECTORS (The Unholy Three)
by Louis Auchincloss

Eight short stories about men and women subconsciously drawn to self-punishment. By the author of *The Rector of Justin.* (#P2676—60¢)

JULIAN *by Gore Vidal*

A novel about the fourth century Emperor later known as "the Apostate"—who tried to reinstate pagan worship in Christian Rome. A bestseller in its hardcover edition. (#Q2563—95¢)

CEREMONY IN LONE TREE *by Wright Morris*

The hero of the award-winning *The Field of Vision* joins his family in a nostalgic celebration of his ninetieth birthday. (#P2182—60¢)

THE
FIELD
OF
VISION

WRIGHT MORRIS

72054

A SIGNET BOOK

Published by THE NEW AMERICAN LIBRARY

© 1956 BY WRIGHT MORRIS

Published as a SIGNET BOOK
by arrangement with Harcourt, Brace & World, Inc.,
who have authorized this softcover edition.

THIRD PRINTING

SIGNET TRADEMARK REG. U.S. PAT. OFF. AND FOREIGN COUNTRIES
REGISTERED TRADEMARK—MARCA REGISTRADA
HECHO EN CHICAGO, U.S.A.

SIGNET BOOKS are published by
The New American Library, Inc.
1301 Avenue of the Americas, New York, New York 10019

PRINTED IN THE UNITED STATES OF AMERICA

FOR

WINONA

AND I PROMISED YOU A SHIP

WITH A GOLDEN MAST

The mind is its own place, and in itself
Can make a Heav'n of Hell, a Hell of Heav'n.
John Milton
Paradise Lost

You mustn't look in my novel for the old stable
ego of the character. There is another ego, according to whose action the individual is unrecognizable, and passes through, as it were, allotropic states which it needs a deeper sense than any we've been used to exercise, to discover are states of the same single radically unchanged element.
D. H. Lawrence

McKee

The seat in the shady side of the bullring made McKee cold. *Sol* would have been better, as they called it, but McKee had wanted the best. Tell him we want the best, he had said to Boyd, but that turned out to be shade. The people over in the sun, however, looked a lot more comfortable. They were drinking cold beer, and they sat there in the sun with their shirt sleeves rolled. It just went to prove, McKee reflected, if you didn't really know what the best was, the smart thing to do was not stick out your neck and ask for it. Not in Mexico. Not if what you really wanted was a seat in the *sol*.

When they came out of the tunnel into the bullring McKee had felt a little dizzy, took a grip on the rail. Same feeling he got watching motorcycles spin in one of those wooden bowls. "We going to sit right smack down on the drain?" he had said, since that was how the bullring itself really looked. Small. Just a round hole at the bottom of a concrete bowl. And these seats they had were right on the lip of it. Cold as a street curb the moment the sun went down. Between the seats these iron bars as smooth as a pump handle, and just about as cold as a pump handle in the winter time. McKee had put his hand on one and said—turning to his grandson he had said—"Cold enough, bygolly, to freeze your tongue to a pump handle." You wouldn't believe it, but that boy didn't know what a pump handle was. Not knowing that he naturally couldn't grasp what McKee meant. To make it worse, when McKee explained it he couldn't get it through his head why anyone with any sense would stick his

7

tongue to one. "You go ask your Uncle Boyd—" McKee had said, just to get rid of him. He didn't know what to make of a boy like that.

Not that he wanted to complain. About the weather, that is. It was on the cool side in the shade, but not cold. Whereas it was eight or ten below back where they came from. Probably colder, since the Omaha paper tended to minimize the weather. People wouldn't cross the state of Nebraska at all if they knew how cold it was. They would go through South Dakota, which was even worse, but south of North Dakota so it sounded warmer. Mexico sounded hot, but that was due to the food. McKee himself would have preferred Hawaii, but that would have meant going off without their grandson, whereas by traveling in the car they could take both the boy and his great-granddaddy. They could have gone to Florida, for that matter, where they could have seen people who talked their own language, but maybe even fewer who were willing to shut up and just listen to it. But as he often said to Mrs. McKee, you could count on the fingers of one hand the people who knew what it was they wanted, or meant what they said. And she knew who he meant. You couldn't pull the wool over Mrs. McKee.

Take what he'd said to Boyd. When he had run into Boyd in the Sanborn's lobby, Boyd had said, "How are you, McKee?" and what had he replied? That he couldn't be happier. *Mrs. McKee and me couldn't be happier.* That's what he had said. The moment he had said it he knew something about it didn't sound quite right. If he'd been asked by anybody but Gordon Boyd he would have said it and very likely believed it, but he always wondered if he meant what he said to Boyd. So did Mrs. McKee.

"These seats remind you of anything, Lois?" he

said, since they reminded McKee of something. The time they went to see Boyd's play in Omaha. Had these reserved front seats since it was Boyd's play, and didn't cost him anything. Play purported to be about a walk on the water the young man in the play planned to get around to, but there was no more on the stage than there was in the bullring. Maybe less. In the bullring at least there was sand, which was what the play called for, since the water was in this sandpit east of Polk. But on the stage in Omaha there was nothing but talk. McKee had found most of it hard to follow. He was the only man alive, besides Boyd, himself, who had been there at the sandpit when it all happened, but the scenery wasn't there, and without the scenery it didn't make sense. What sort of sandpit can you have on an empty stage? The strangest thing McKee had ever set his eyes on, a lot stranger than ghosts or flying saucers, had been a person like Boyd thinking he could do something like that. Listening to a lot of talk, in an auditorium, about a boy who was *thinking* of walking on water, had nothing to do with being out at a sandpit, and seeing it done. Seeing it tried, that is. Seeing him come within an ace of drowning himself. The strange thing wasn't so much that he tried—it was what you might expect of a person with a screw loose—but that right up till he failed, till he dropped out of sight, McKee had almost believed it himself. It was that sort of thing people talking on a stage couldn't bring out. It wasn't only Boyd who was crazy, and believed it. McKee had believed it himself.

"Don't remind you of a sandpit, does it?" he said, since the bullring struck him as quite a bit like one. A dry one. The way he'd like to see every sandpit. Without the water there no kid would feel he had to walk on it.

"No, it *does not* remind me of a sandpit," she replied.

In her opinion, especially when they traveled, McKee was always being reminded of something. That is to say, everything reminded him of something else. The outside of this bullring, for instance, reminded McKee of the Lincoln Library basement. Of the big framed pictures on the walls of the basement, Roman ruins, the Coliseum, places like that. McKee had never been to Rome himself, but he had raised a boy who had lived in that basement. The ruins that looked like the bullring were over in the corner where he usually sat. The boy's name was Gordon. Named after Gordon Boyd, that is. Grown up and married now, with four youngsters of his own, the oldest one right there in the bullring with them, sitting right beside Boyd, the man who had almost ruined his daddy's life. Back at that time his daddy, Gordon McKee, had been just about as crazy as Boyd had been, a moody stage-struck kid who would have tried to walk on air, if the play called for it. He might not have almost drowned himself, like Boyd, but he would have been up in the air all his life if they hadn't made that trip back to New York, where he saw Boyd. Where he saw, that is, what was left of him. The great man in his life looking no different than a common bum. When the boy saw what it was like to walk on water—what it was like, that is, if you failed—he at least had sense enough, which he got from his mother, to give it up. You didn't have to rub his nose in his own mess to make him see the point.

"Anybody want a cool drink?" said McKee, and leaned forward, his hands on the rail, to look down the row to the man at the end of it. Gordon Boyd. He could look right at him since the row was curved. But he wouldn't have known it, or guessed it, if he hadn't been told. Big and soft now, almost the yellow color of the Mexicans. Habit of stroking his face, one side, as though he thought he might need a shave. Next to him was the boy, McKee's grandson, wearing his coonskin hat and Davy Crockett outfit, and in a coonskin hat right there beside him was the old man. Not a real coonskin, an imitation with a stringy tail that wouldn't fool anybody, but the old man was so blind all he could do was feel it, and it felt like a tail. McKee had never openly said, nor did he like to think, that his wife's father had a screw loose somewhere, although everybody said so and he knew it himself everytime he looked at him. Now that he was eighty-seven they could blame it on his age, but the screw that was loose had been loose from the beginning. His own wife—a woman with a lot of horse sense—had been the first to point it out. He didn't really live in this world, as she put it, but he left her with a string of kids to raise in it, and one of those kids, as it turned out, was McKee's wife. She didn't look much like her father, but she had his pale blue eyes, and let her get a little riled and you could see his jaw jutting out of her face.

Next to him was Mrs. Kahler, a woman whose eyes were as good as McKee's, if not better, but due to some mental trouble she saw very little out of them. If McKee understood it, she saw only what she wanted to see. Here at the bullfight, for instance, she didn't seem to see the bulls. They just brought her along because she liked the music and the company. First thing McKee felt, when he set eyes on her, was how long it had been since he had seen George Arliss, since she had the sort of face, homely but friendly, that you like right off the bat. She liked to knit at the bullfight, and was knitting Dr. Lehmann a pair of red sox. He was right beside her. She had already knit him the mittens he was wearing, and the red wool scarf.

If there was one thing that made McKee tired, it was to hear people say that Nebraska was flat. Lehmann had said so. A foreigner to boot. McKee could show him, both around Polk and Lincoln, as lovely rolling country as he'd ever set eyes on, but it wasn't the Alps, it wasn't the Riviera, and the people weren't busy making cuckoo clocks. As he understood they were back where Lehmann came from, wherever that was. Boyd himself had once said, and McKee had never forgotten it, that Switzerland was like a national park where they let the cows run on the golf course to keep the grass short. Dr. Leopold Lehmann, like those foreign types McKee had met in Omaha and Lincoln, didn't seem to feel at home if he wasn't at the bottom or the top of something. Nebraska hardly ever went up and down like that. But if you'd take a little place like the Swiss Alps, which was all up and down, and put it through a roller, some sort of open country, like they had around Lincoln, was what you'd get. Which was just about what, if McKee understood it, that big sheet of ice did when it covered Nebraska, leaving these little sandpits where kids like McKee and Boyd could drown.

Sandpits always gave McKee the willies, which was why the empty bullring made him so uneasy, as if they were all just sitting there waiting for the water to rise. When it reached a certain level, some fool kid would try to walk on it. If you got as many people as there were present sitting around a little hole in the ground, like this ring was, it just naturally followed that something would happen. Almost anything. Where you had so many people a wild streak would turn up in one of them.

McKee looked for it where he had once seen it. The face of Gordon Boyd. He didn't look so well. On the other hand, he didn't really look sick. It was hard to judge a man who left egg on his front and drove all over Mexico in a '38 Ford coupe. McKee would like to know if he was sick upstairs, which was why he was down here with this Dr. Lehmann, or if they were doing some sort of book together, as he seemed to imply. If their seats had been closer he would have asked. He could talk to Boyd. After all, there was nobody who knew him so well, nobody who had seen him up and down the ladder, and who liked him any more than McKee—if that was the word. It probably wasn't. If he had to name it, it seldom was. Whatever the word was, when he saw this tourist in the Sanborn's lobby, with his fly unzipped, he had felt no compunction—as he ordinarily would have—about speaking to him. He didn't know this tourist from Adam—what he felt was, when he began to feel something, that it was an old feeling and he had felt it many times before. He recognized the feeling. After that he recognized the man. The feeling—which hadn't changed, and in respect to the feeling the man hadn't either—was that he'd never notice anything was wrong. McKee would have to. McKee would have to tap him on the shoulder, lean forward, and speak the word *fly*. The responsibility—*that* was the feeling—had always rested with McKee, in such matters, since Boyd had always lacked what McKee had been born with, good horse sense. He had never had it. He had even done without it—while he had McKee. The real trouble—if the truth were known, but of course it wouldn't be, and perhaps it shouldn't—the real trouble began when McKee was no longer there. When he could no longer, in the plainest sense, be responsible. Keep an eye on his wild streak, his fly, or whatever it was. When he went off to that school in the East, where he turned up, suddenly, famous—and when he turned up in Lincoln, needing McKee, it was too late. McKee had his own Gordon Boyd by then. He had to run his own life. He had a woman on his hands who would almost whoop-up if he mentioned Boyd. He did what he could, both then and later; McKee gave him a son he knew he would never have, and in going that far he amost ruined all of their lives. All except Boyd's. *He* had taken care of that all by himself.

The last time they'd seen Boyd—Mrs. McKee hadn't seen him, just McKee, the boy, his Uncle Roy and Aunt Agnes—had been in '39 when they all drove to New York for the World's Fair. In one of those doughnut shops around Times Square Agnes had thought of Boyd, found his name in the phone book, and the upshot of it was they had all gone down to this loft where he lived. They found him up there with his shirt off, no furniture to speak of, nobody anywhere around to look after him, and this fool ball-player's pocket lying on his desk. One he'd torn off Ty Cobb's pants, way back when he was a kid. McKee had been with him the time he did it—the way he'd been with him out at the sandpit—but who would have dreamed he would have hung on to a soiled rag like that? Twenty-five years. When Agnes asked him why it was he still had it, he said it was the only thing he hadn't lost his grip on. Everything else he got his hands on, he said, he'd dropped. It had been just pitiful to hear him say it, and to see the truth in it, but it had been a life-saver for the boy, Gordon, to see it for himself. He saw exactly where it was the sort of life he was leading led. Except for Boyd, and that fool pocket, he might not have married and settled down. And McKee's grandson, this little tyke in the bullring, might not have been born. A boy they also called Gordon, after his father; but the name really belonged to Boyd, and McKee often wondered if it hadn't been the name that ruined Boyd's own life.

If there had ever been anything like a real misunderstanding between McKee and his wife, it had been when he named his first-born son Gordon, after Boyd. They'd made an arrangement, the way young people do until they get older, and know better, that if it was going to be a girl, she would name it, whereas if it was a boy she would leave it to McKee. So he named him Gordon. That was not only what they named him, but who he was.

The other two *she* named, to see if she could get even, one of them Seward after an uncle, and the other one Orien since she had been hoping it might be a girl. And yet the boy who started off worst, and gave them nothing but trouble, was the first to settle down and now gave them the least. After being stage-struck for more than two years, chasing around with girls who were crazier than he was, he turned up married to a good solid girl they hadn't known he'd even met, from a part of the state they hadn't known he'd ever been in. His father-in-law, O. P. Rideout, of Chadron, settled eight thousand head of steer on them the day they were married, and it might have been the weight of all that beef that calmed the boy down. Mr. Rideout himself, who had raised five boys, said it often turned out that the first pup in the litter, meaning one like Gordon, tended to run a little wild. Lead dog, as he put it, had nothing to follow but his own scent. But Gordon did. In fact, it was the scent that threw him off. Threw them all off, just a little, since there was something about Boyd, besides the scent he gave off, that got people to acting as if they didn't know their own minds. Which they usually didn't. Mrs. McKee had said as much herself.

Take the way he acted when McKee recognized him. He hadn't set eyes on Boyd for fifteen years, but the first thing he said, without any introduction, was—

"McKee, how's the little woman?"

It wasn't till he heard *that* that McKee was sure just who he was. McKee had said she was fine, just fine, remembering in time not to ask about *his* wife, which he usually made considerable effort to do, just to be polite. As he had to say something, McKee had inquired what in the world had brought him to Mexico.

"All Gaul's divided into three parts," Boyd had replied, "Juvenile, Mobile and Senile delinquents. I'm in the Mobile division. How are things with you?"

Right there, in a nutshell, you had everything that was wrong with him. The way he'd keep you guessing. The way you couldn't be sure where the devil you stood. Mrs. McKee had pointed out, even before she met him, and long before it got to be popular, that just hearing about Boyd gave her a feeling of insecurity. The way she put it was, the ground didn't seem solid beneath her feet. Anything might happen with a person like that, and he had gone out of his way to prove her right. It had almost happened, according to her, the first time she met him. Boyd had kissed her. Up till then she'd never been kissed.

In answer to his question McKee had said that he and Mrs. McKee couldn't be happier. Reason he did, of course, was to reassure Boyd on that point. Then he mentioned Gordon, the big cattle ranch he had, and how the boy—when he heard where they were going —asked him to keep an eye peeled for a nice pair of bulls. The boy had said oxen, not bulls, since he was thinking of breeding a strain of them, but when McKee got to that point he heard himself say *nice pair of fighting bulls*. What had struck him? An example of what Boyd did to him. To all of them. Just to keep in the running with a person like Boyd they had to stretch the point, in so far as they had one, and a fighting bull was what McKee got when he stretched an ox. One thing led to another, after that, with Boyd offering to take him out to the bullring, and McKee trying to act as if he wasn't flabbergasted. What he said was, naturally, that he'd have to speak to the little woman, since the bullfight was the one thing she didn't like about Mexico. She hadn't seen one, but it just made her sick to know they took place. McKee would have bet the shirt off his back that she would refuse to set her eyes on Boyd, let alone be seen at something like a bullfight with him. That was where he was wrong. That was where he never knew about Mrs. McKee. She'd been simply horrified that he could even suggst it—just hearing Boyd was alive had sort of upset her—which was why McKee hadn't stepped to the phone and called it off. Then they went to lunch, and before lunch was over she'd changed her mind. The only reason Boyd had even brought it up, she said, was that he knew it would upset her, which naturally placed her under the obligation to go. Once she saw it in that light, of course, they went. McKee had bought the tickets, priced about the same as a Big League game back in the States, with the center of the bullring about as far away as the pitcher's mound. Right smack in the center, like a big Maypole, they had this giant Pepsi-Cola bottle, which was the way they advertised things in Mexico. It made McKee smile. It also reminded him of something else.

"Anybody like a cool *soft* drink?" he said, just in case his wife's father got any fancy ideas. Whatever the old man had, they would have to give the boy. Eight and eighty, but alike as two peas in a pod.

McKee watched the boy shoot up his hand, then aim his plastic six-shooter at the Pepsi-Cola bottle. The idea of a soft drink like that in a bullring made McKee smile. He felt it called for hard ones. He found it hard to believe they'd soon be killing a bull where a bottle like that advertised Pepsi-Cola. On the other hand, he didn't feel so bad about bringing the boy. It couldn't be too bad if people sat around drinking something like pop. Boyd had said he didn't need to worry about the boy since kids liked blood and just loved to poke an eye out. That was like Boyd. He wanted to shock Mrs. McKee, and that was just what he did. But she'd made up her mind she was going to sit through it if for no other reason than Boyd thought she couldn't. He hadn't yet learned that you couldn't scare a woman like Mrs. McKee.

"Hey you!" McKee said, and wagged his hand at one of the boys with soft drinks in a bucket. Boyd *pssssst* at them, which sounded like hissing, but Mc-Kee didn't want to pick up that sort of habit. If he hissed at kids selling pop in the States, they'd throw the bottle at him. This kid came up with his pail, the bottles floating in water, and took the cap from one of the Pepsi bottles. He looked to be about the same sort of boy McKee saw around Lincoln, in the poorer sections. He wore a striped paper hat, advertising something, and it crossed McKee's mind that it might be paint.

"Pintura mean paint, Lois?" he said, and out the corner of his eye he saw her head nodding. Back at Thanksgiving—when Mrs. McKee had made up her mind she had to go somewhere, or go crazy—she had got these Spanish records, since that was what they talked in Mexico. But a week or so of listening to that had almost led McKee to think he'd rather go crazy. He got so he almost hated the man on the record— just his voice, since he never really saw him—and he hated the woman who was Señora somebody, and her two dam kids. The only word he really learned was *agua*, which turned out to be worse than useless, since *agua* was the one thing nobody even touched in Mexico. They drank *cerveza*, which was beer, or any-thing in big bottles, like Pepsi-Cola.

Not that McKee didn't sort of like Mexico. In the four days they had been in Mexico City ten or twelve people had asked him for the time, then thanked him kindly no matter what it was he said. He liked that. He paid a little more attention to the time himself.

Having it there in his pocket meant more down here than it did in the States.

"Here you are, son," he said, passing along the bottle, and when Boyd reached for it he added, "See that hat the kid's wearing is a paint hat. Guess old Sherwin Williams still covers the world."

"Coffers wot?" said Dr. Lehmann, and put a red mittened hand to his ear. McKee had thought the old man was crazy to wear a pair of wool mittens to a bullfight, but he could see he wasn't. Not in what they called the *sombra*. McKee would have preferred hot coffee to pop. Dr. Lehmann had a wool lap robe across his knees, and between his hands, that is, the red mittens, he held a silver flask that had a tiny cup for a cap. He took a snifter now and then, Boyd had said, for medicinal purposes. He was old. His circulation wasn't so good. "Coffers—?" Lehmann repeated, eyeing McKee, since he was a foreigner and didn't quite catch that.

"It's a house paint," said Boyd, reaching for the bottle. "Company that sold the paint used to give away hats. Had them when we were kids. Looks like the same old line down here."

Dr. Lehmann smiled as if he grasped that. McKee doubted that he did. Using the heel of his palm, his back to Mrs. McKee, McKee honed the spout to the bottle, then tried to take a swallow without tipping back his head. It didn't work, but it made him think of something.

"And now what?" said Mrs. McKee, who never missed a trick. Even at a bullfight. Back in Lincoln McKee would have the fork in his mouth, or the bottle to his lips, then he would stop as though it was poisoned. But when she asked him what in the world the trouble was, he hardly ever knew. She asked him now, and he said—

"Just thought of something."

He meant reminded, of course, but it wasn't a word he could use. But when he'd half tipped his head, when he'd got his eyes closed, he saw a whole bunch of kids wearing those fool paint hats. He could see the paint hats, that is, but he couldn't see who the kids were. Like all the paint hats he'd ever seen, they were too big for a kid. These kids were snorting up and down like Indians, some of them with knives, some with pieces of bottle, which if you got it to break just right made a pretty good blade. What was going on? Aloud, McKee said—

"Gordon, you ever shoot a hog?"

Although he knew he hadn't. Just woodpeckers. As a boy he took the line they were bad for the trees.

"A *hog?*" said Boyd. "When was this?"

It pleased McKee to hear him ask it. He didn't answer right away for two reasons. He had to think again himself when it was that had happened, and once he had thought he didn't want to spoil it. He never had much to offer. He had to keep from blurting it out.

"Year you was away," said McKee, and let *him* figure out when that was. McKee had gone to Texas, and Boyd had gone to a school in the East somewhere.

"This was in Polk?" asked Boyd.

"Nope," said McKee, "this was in Texas."

"This was *where?*" said Boyd, since that was what he said if he liked what you told him. McKee held on. He took a mouthful of the pop. As if it didn't really matter where he spent the winter, he spit it out.

"This was where in Texas?" said Boyd, and McKee replied—

"Near Amarillo."

Surprised, once he said it, that he still remembered it. How long? Almost forty years. In his mind's eye, bigger than life, he could see the state of Texas. A sea without water in it. Anyhow, that was how he felt about it himself. But he knew better than say that to Boyd, so he said—

"Down there with my Uncle Dwight. Guess he invented the dust bowl." Although he really hadn't. All that winter he had had McKee's help.

"Christ!" said Boyd. "I didn't know you had an uncle."

Shamelessly, McKee gulped down half the pop. Too fast, so that the fizz backed up. He belched.

"Tastes good both ways," he said, since that was why *they* used to do it. When they did it, that was what *they* said. Boyd's idea. McKee tried to think— turning over in his mind what he remembered about his uncle—if there was anything about him that Boyd might admire. A very strange man. McKee never knew where he got the idea of raising wheat. Down there, that is. Where nothing like wheat had been grown before. Panhandle grassland that had never been turned by a plow. But they had turned it—he and McKee had turned it—and the first swirling clouds of dust had begun to blow. When it had darkened the sun over places like New York, McKee had thought of that.

"Guess we stirred up the dust bowl between us," he said, and for all of that they might have.

"You're not kidding?" replied Boyd. Which meant that he believed it. He doubted everything, as a rule, but he was free to believe anything he wanted.

"Think we did," said McKee, soberly, and ran his tongue along his gums; up front, that is, just the way he used to when they were covered with a film of dust. Think of that. He could almost taste it after forty years. All the time he was in Texas his teeth had looked rotted because of the mud caked around the roots, the way dirt would pack hard and black around the foot of a post. Nothing would budge it.

"So you shot this hog—?" said Boyd, wanting to get on.

Bigger than life, McKee could see him. Looked as big or bigger to him then than a bull did now. He'd been in the pen with him. He could almost touch his snout with the barrel of the gun. Reason the hog had moved in so close was that he'd waddled over to where he could smell, as well as see, the ear of yellow corn McKee had in the front of his pants. Sticking out of his fly. Which was why, come to think, he had never mentioned it.

"Shot him right between the eyes," went on McKee, and put up his little finger to indicate the hole size.

"He have three eyes then?" said the boy.

"That's just what he did," said McKee.

"Two to look out, and one to look in, eh?" said Boyd.

"I do believe there is a limit," said Mrs. McKee, but before she reached it they all heard this racket. A bugle? It pulled, like the suck of a lemon, at McKee's ears. Way up behind him, up the slope that made him nearly dizzy when he turned and looked at it, way up there where they let them all sit for three pesos he could see the band. But just trying to look made him feel like he was spinning. Was it the rows of hats? There was no sun behind him, but every one of those Mexicans had a straw hat. Made the slope as shiny as a tile roof. He watched one go sailing off. The noise the band made poured down on them and McKee felt heavy, as if the music was like water. It pulled the way the tub drain did when the plug slipped out.

"Granpa!" yelled the boy. "Look, granpa!" and Mc-Kee wheeled around, his hands gripping the rail, to watch men who looked like midgets going off with the Pepsi bottle. They looked like circus dwarfs with that bottle, and confirmed McKee's feeling of some basic disorder. Some disproportion that made him feel

a little unbalanced, unsure of himself. The way he'd
feel if he landed on the moon, or felt drawn to it. He
watched the men, all of them so many midgets, and it
crossed his mind what was wrong with it. Back in the
States they'd have a truck, or some machine, to take
care of that. But people—pretty little ones at that—
still did the work in Mexico. On the highway coming
down they'd crossed an iron bridge that looked like it
was crawling with hundreds of insects, but on closer
inspection they turned out to be Indians. Full grown
ones. What were they up to? They were chipping the
rust off that fool bridge with sharp pointed rocks.
Coming on them like that McKee had had the feeling
that his eyes were slipping, or that liquid was in his ear
drums, since the scale of the thing, like the men with
the bottle, threw him off. They took it out through a
gate where McKee could see, when they got the gates
wide open, a bunch of young men who looked like
trapeze artists in tights. All men. No pretty girl to lead
off swinging her baton. Then he caught sight, just
before the gates closed, of a dark horse and a black
frocked rider. A somber note. Was he going to be
part of the same parade? He thought he'd ask Boyd,
and leaned over to do it, tapping his bottle on the rail
to attract Boyd's attention, when the gates swung
wide and this fellow on the horse pranced into the ring.
All by himself, the horse a high fancy stepper, but as
if they both forgot the parade was behind them, and
they'd gone off not knowing they were out there all
alone.

"See that, Lois?" said McKee, since what it made
him think of was her father. Whether he had a screw
loose or not, he could handle a horse. This dark horse
and his rider came right at them, clear across the ring
without a thing behind them, then stopped right there
below them, where the rider doffed his black hat. He
said a few words—McKee turned to see who it was he

had his eye on—but when he turned back he could hardly believe his eyes. Both horse and rider were backing up. Anybody who had ever tried to back up a horse could appreciate that. Clear across the ring, maybe a good hundred yards, every inch of it backwards to the gate he had come in, where the young men in their tights, and the rest of the parade, were waiting for him.

"Know what happened?" said McKee, nudging his wife's elbow. "He meant to bring 'em along, but he forgot to hitch 'em up. Got clean over here before he noticed he was alone."

Over his mouth, to indicate he was laughing, McKee cupped his hand. Mrs. McKee said nothing. She didn't even trouble to edge away from him. Which meant she felt it too, whatever it was, since when she felt something pretty strong, she froze up, whereas McKee always tried to say something good for a laugh.

And then, without really knowing why, he stood up. Got to his feet as though the national anthem was being played. "Here they come!" he said, as if she couldn't see it, and then like a fool he took off his straw hat. The one he'd bought for just two pesos outside the ring. People thought he did that—as he heard later—so the ladies could see in the row behind him, since the brim of this hat he'd bought was pretty big. Nobody in his own row, luckily, took notice of it. He watched this rider on the dark horse lead the way, which gave it an off-key flavor, but the young men in their tights, and the mules with the pom-poms, made up for it. When they spread out in the ring, so he could see them, he thought all the young men in the front row were injured, since they carried their left arms in a sort of sling. But it hardly seemed likely they'd all been bull-struck on the same arm. It was part of the parade, the curious way they did things, like having that sad looking black horse leading, and the slinky sort of way they all seemed to march, sticking out their hips. The music was sharp, but not the way they marched to it. Fairly good-looking boys in other respects, with a row of older men right behind them, some of them a little fat in the midriff and the rear for bullfighting. From the pictures he'd seen, it didn't strike McKee as the place to stick out. Right behind the men were the mules, with their pom-poms, then these fellows with outfits like street cleaners, and from what they brought along with them, maybe that was what they were. Wheelbarrows, shovels, brooms, and that sort of thing. They came along behind the mules, and McKee thought that was good. Charlie Chaplin had made a mighty funny movie out of something like that. The point was good, if McKee got it, but what interested him most were the mules, since he wondered if these were the horses everybody complained about. Had it reached the point where people couldn't tell a mule from a horse?

"Boyd—" he said, and leaned forward to ask him, when he happened to notice the rear end of the horses. Two of them, looking like upholstered furniture. A little fat-bottomed man sat on each of them. It seemed hard to believe he hadn't seen such a sight when it came right at him, but he hadn't, and it should teach him, only it wouldn't, to keep his mouth closed.

"What are the mules for?" he said, since he had to say something.

"The mules drack oaf the det bools," said Dr. Lehmann.

"*Bulls?*" said McKee, since it hadn't crossed his mind there'd be several of them. Nor had it crossed his mind what they did with any of them. It wasn't a bullfight. It was a *bulls* fight. For the first time he wondered if he was going to like it. In a cheery voice he said—

"Well, folks, what's next on the bill?"

Someone shouted right behind him, like he meant to tell him, but when McKee turned all the hands waved at him; feeling a tug on his sleeve he glanced at Mrs. McKee. She pulled him down. Right there before him, as if he'd come in with the parade but they'd gone off without him, was the bull.

McKee thought he looked small.

Mrs. McKee

Dr. Lehmann's breath—he was that close—had the sweetish smell of furniture polish from the lozenge she could see, green as a horse's bit, when he opened his mouth. He was saying—his language was so garbled she hardly knew what he was saying—if she hadn't read it all, nearly every word of it, somewhere else. How the parade, this procession they had seen, was a parable of life. The heroes at the front—he had said *sheroes*, but that was due to the lozenge—and ahead of them, a portent, the horseman who wore black. A somber foreboding of what lay ahead in the hero's life. And then the riffraff—he had used the word riffraff, indicating his foreign extraction—the riffraff, the mules, and the men with brooms and shovels who cleaned up the mess. All of this he had recited as if he had thought it up himself. But the night before, in the little book McKee had smiled at her for buying, *Toros without Tears*, she had read the same thing but much better put. Not the riffraff, no, that was his own, or the idea of people cleaning up the mess, but that the procession had allegorical elements. Something that hardly needed, she would have said, pointing out.

If only her mother could have seen the man on the horse. Coming in alone like that, like her father, not caring if the parade was or wasn't behind him, making his little speech, then backing out of the picture. Just like that.

"When the century turned, darling," her mother had said, with a sour look, "your father didn't." He not only didn't turn, he backed right out of it. For almost forty years there was nothing that pleased him, nothing that he either cared to live or die for, which had a good deal to do with the fact that he was neither alive nor dead. One of those people she had read about somewhere who could sleep with their eyes wide open, and, like this Mrs. Kahler, look through them without seeing anything.

Nobody knew, for instance, if her father was as good as blind, or not. He wouldn't answer simple questions. He wouldn't look through the glasses doctors tried on him. If he had no common sense he seemed to have all the others—he could scoot around like a bug when he cared to—or he would just sit as though every muscle in his body was paralyzed. The way he sat now. Absolutely determined not to see anything. She had had to lead him in like a blind man, poking at everything with that cane he carried, looking like some sort of clown in the silly coonskin hat. He knew perfectly well the impression he was making and that she looked like a fool; that is to say, they all did, coming to a bullfight with a poor old man who was blind as a bat. "What froze him up?" McKee has said, as if it was something she had done herself. Her father had frozen up the moment the boy began to talk to Boyd. Which meant that it was now absolutely hopeless since the child ignored him completely, and acted just as if he had lived all of his life with Boyd. Nothing had changed. It made her flesh crawl just to think of it.

"You cold, Lois?" said McKee. "You got goose pimples."

Naturally, she didn't hear that. If she let on that she heard it he would take off his coat—showing his elastic garter-type arm bands—since he would take off his coat at the slightest provocation here in Mexico. Before he had it so much as draped around her shoulders, he would start sneezing himself.

Not that she was cold. Anyhow, not so cold as she looked. She looked at her hands—one of them dark brown from the sun on the side of the car she had sat on—but both of them, as she knew without her glasses, jittery. The pyramid? Let them call it the pyramid. She had gone up the pyramid: many people did, but it had been ill-advised in her case, since she had to take injections to quiet her down, then pills to pep her up. The pills made her so nervous that something in the mattress, the springs, or the straw in her pillow, made a crackling sound that kept her awake all night. On top of that she had set eyes on Boyd, something that always unnerved her, and to make matters worse here she was with him in an actual bullring. She tipped forward, as if to peer into the runway, what they called the *callejon* in that book she had read, then glanced down the row to the man at the end of it. Was that what tropical nights and Latin women had done to him? She saw it all very clearly, and remembered that she had been the *first*.

Walter McKee could see the goose flesh on her arms very easily, but he had once stood, like a wooden Indian, and watched his best friend be the first man to kiss his future bride. What McKee had felt she couldn't imagine, but she would never forget what it had done to the bride. It had affected her—now that she had made it—like the pyramid climb. Queasy in her middle. Her legs trembling when she was lying down. Just to be witty Boyd had said that the arms of girls made him think of folding chairs, the easy way they would bend backward, and for weeks she had suffered from the notion that her own arms might. This habit she had of hugging herself dated from that time. It kept her elbows bent the *right* way, and covered up how jittery she was. The crazy thing about it was that he had them both—her friend Alice Morple had been there with her—but he had kissed Alice second, so that she had a little time to prepare herself. As McKee himself would verify, Alice had stuck her neck out like a goose. But that was all beside the point, the point being that Boyd had kissed her *first*, and Alice Morple had said, "If you were so surprised, why did you kiss him back?"

She had been too shocked to speak.

"All I've got to say is," Alice Morple had said, which she always put in if it certainly wasn't, "I didn't have time to lick the candied apple off *before* he kissed me."

Then they had gone to bed—Alice Morple was visiting her for the week end—and since they couldn't sleep Alice Morple had naturally made some further remarks. "It was a good thing he went off when he did," she said, laughing as if she was being tickled, and more or less implying that it didn't seem to matter that McKee had been there. Did it? How could she ignore the terrible truth? He had been there on the porch, right there with them, when this boy she had never seen before in her life, although she had heard about him, stepped forward and kissed her smack on the lips. The point being she had known he would. Her own lips were prepared. They had been eating candied apple and she had put out her tongue and licked the sticky part off.

Then came the dream—but she wouldn't go into that. She hadn't slept a wink that night or the next one, her knees would almost knock when she stooped for something, and she felt all over like the hum the wires make in a telephone pole. If McKee or Alice Morple touched her, it would make her jump. It wasn't in her mind at all, like the books say, but a current all over her body and a feeling that if she touched something it would spark. Somewhere near her middle a buzzing sensation, as if she had swallowed a fly. For two or three weeks she was like one of the chickens who had eaten the laying mash that had soured, his head off to one side, walking around like he was on thin air. Nothing he managed to put his foot on felt right to him. What he had taken for granted as solid ground was more like air. He didn't trust his own senses, or anybody else's, and McKee had pointed out it was a fine example of what fermented spirits would do to anyone. But without fermented spirits, just a candied apple, she had been in the same condition as the chicken; she didn't trust her own senses, and the ground kept shifting beneath her feet. She had just enough wit to do what she could. She married Mc-Kee.

She also took it for granted that he understood *something*, since he had been there, and saw what had happened, but when their first child was born what did he do but name it after Boyd. So he had been there, but he hadn't seen a thing. McKee was the kindest person in the world, but he never saw more, when he looked at her, than whether she had migraine or goosepimples on her arms or not. He would never see more than he could cover up by taking off his coat. When he called her on the hotel telephone and said, "Lois, you'd never guess who I just ran into—" her body had been crawling with goosepimples before she heard. *It* knew, even before *she* did, and in that respect nothing had changed since she had licked the candied apple from her lips more than thirty years ago. Not that he would want to kiss her now, or she would let him, but the knowledge that her body knew what she didn't, and would not let her forget it, was exactly the same. Anything might happen. And once it almost did.

Until that night she hadn't set eyes on Boyd, but

she had heard about him from the morning that Mc-
Kee, who had an egg route then, had stepped into her
aunt's kitchen to thaw himself out. He'd made a joke
about the chickens being frozen in the shell, which
got them all to laughing, then he said it wasn't really
his joke, but one he'd heard in Omaha. Her aunt said,
had he really been to Omaha? And McKee had said
he had, he had been there for Christmas, which he had
spent with his old friend Gordon Boyd. She had
been just fifteen at the time, which meant McKee was
seventeen, since he was two years older, but it seemed
strange to hear him refer to his *old friend*, Gordon
Boyd. He hardly ever said Gordon. He always said
Gordon Boyd. When she knew him better, and asked
him why it was he never talked about himself, only
about this Gordon, it hadn't crossed his mind there
was anything else to talk about. When it did, he
thought it over then said that Gordon Boyd, his
old friend, was half an orphan. His father had died
before he had really set eyes on him. It hadn't been
McKee's fault, but he seemed to feel responsible for
him. Other people he knew felt the same way; a family
named Crete, who were very wealthy, and when their
own boy died they more or less adopted Gordon
Boyd. He lived with them in Omaha, where they
had better schools, and long before the New York
theater people knew about him Mrs. Crete put up the
money and made the people she knew come to see
his plays. One of them was a talent scout, from the
East, and although nobody in Omaha could believe
it, the crazy play he wrote about the sandpit had made
a big hit in New York. Otherwise she and McKee
might never have seen it. At that, it was almost
twenty years; then the WPA revived it, and her own
son, who was stage-struck at the time, played the
leading role. Doing all of those things, that is, pre-
tending to do them, that Gordon Boyd had done

nearly twenty years before him, such as brazenly kissing the girl, the fiancee, of his own best friend. He knew just what he was doing, and from there went off and drowned himself. Not intentionally, but with the full understanding that if he failed to walk on the water, which he naturally did, it would prove that he was not truly worthy of her.

There was of course more to it, everybody talked for hours, but as McKee himself told her later, none of it was made up—Boyd had once tried to walk on water, and nearly drowned. It was certainly just like him, as Alice Morple said, to write a play where he could take full credit for drowning, but still be around, in the lobby somewhere, and able to enjoy it. The meaning of the play, so far as she could understand it, was that if he had managed to walk on the water he would have come back and run off with the girl he had just kissed. The same night. While the taste, as he said, of the candied apple was still on her lips. The point being that the girl, all of this time, was sitting up and waiting for him.

"Know what happened?" said McKee, and she almost blurted that *nothing* had happened, which was the trouble, but he wasn't directing the question to her, but to Boyd. He waved his arm at the horse and rider, said—"He meant to bring 'em along, but he forgot to hitch 'em up. Got clean over here before he noticed he was alone."

He brought his hand down hard on her knee, as if it was his own. It was something he normally wouldn't think of doing, and she knew, from the way he did it, that he was as jittery and queasy in the middle as she was herself. Was it the altitude? He had climbed no pyramid. Or was it something that Gordon Boyd did to both of them? She had always been so upset herself—the two or three times she had seen Boyd—there had hardly been a chance to see how he affected

McKee. Now she could see it was the same. If you asked him, he probably couldn't tell you *where* he was. He was acting like a clown to cover up how nervous he was. Was it all one way? Didn't Boyd ever feel very much himself? She turned her head, her lips tight to keep her tongue from misbehaving, and looked at the face of the first man to kiss her. He looked sad. It seemed strange, but that was how he looked. Had such a large sad man actually tried to walk on water at one time? How many girls, on how many other porches, had he kissed? But married none. As if he *really had* drowned himself. As if—she turned to see what the shouting was about, saw McKee standing, his hat off, facing the rows of people waving at him. She pulled him down—was he so befuddled she was going to have him, as well as the others?—she pulled him down and directed his attention toward the ring. A little bull, a calf she would have said, perplexed to be alone out there, his tail wagging, looked around for the 4-H boy or girl who belonged to him. The one who had brought him in, then forgotten him. One of the men shook a cape out, shouting at him, but that wasn't at all what he wanted, and when another ran at him, trailing the cape on the ground, he turned and trotted for the fence. Over he came, the way she knew he would, just as if McKee had a ripe apple for him, and stood there scratching his chin on the top rail. Like a little sprig of flowers, there were green and white ribbons pinned to his hump.

"That what you call a bull, Gordon?" McKee said, and she might have forgotten, if he hadn't, that it wasn't one of her son's beef cattle, but a bull. That the ribbon on his hump wasn't for a prize he had won. She turned to Boyd—he was standing, holding his Pepsi-Cola bottle like a cocktail shaker, his thumb tight across the top, but she could hear the fizz escape.

She watched him lean over the rail, away over, his soft mid-section folded around it, and using his thumb like a nozzle squirt the fizzing pop into the little bull's face. Did he like it? He put out his blue tongue and licked off his snout. Boyd gave the bottle a shake, then squirted him again.

Everybody who saw that began to laugh—the child, her grandson, was almost screaming—but even people who were older, who knew better, seemed to enjoy it. Those who were farther back stood on their seats to get a better view. Boyd used up one bottle and called for another, which the man across the aisle was quick to hand him, and the bull kept his head on the rail, his tongue slapped on his snout. The bullfighters themselves, if that was what you could call them, stood around with their capes, grinning like small children, and when the bottle was drained she saw Boyd wave his hands like a prize fighter. He faced the crowd, he waved the bottle, he bowed at the waist and blew the ladies kisses, and all the time they were whistling like they did when they weren't doing anything else.

"Guess he hasn't changed much, has he?" said Mc-Kee, and they watched him take one of their grandson's toy pistols and shoot into the air. On her father's face, blind as he was, she saw that he had followed the entire performance, although his gaze remained on the little bull.

"Why, he's hardly more than a calf—" she said, as if that was all there was to see, and settled back in her seat the way she did when a fever turned out to be no more than a common cold.

The old man couldn't believe his eyes—the ones he had—but his ears told him the worst. He could hear the crowd yell and the fizzing squirt of the pop. If anybody had told him he would live to see the day a grown man would stand up and squirt pop at someone—but of course, he didn't. Live to see the day, that is. He'd had sense enough to go blind before he lived to see something like that. But one thing he didn't have sense enough to do was just stay put. Where he belonged, that is. He hadn't had sense enough to live, then die, back in Lone Tree.

When they told Tom Scanlon that his wife had died—his daughter, Lois, was the one to tell him—he had taken a kitchen match from his hat band, bit down on it. He let his daughter wait, then after a while he said, "Loey, what'll the hens do?"

She had replied, "Uncle Roy and Agnes are taking them."

It didn't mean that Scanlon didn't feel death any, or not care about people, or other things they said about him. What it meant was that he seldom felt *much*, so any feeling threw him off. When he thought about the chickens he knew what it was he felt, and that the chickens would feel it even more than he did. But being chickens they might not grasp it. So they would need help. They would miss her. That was what he meant.

Scanlon and his wife had been married forty years, but they had not lived more than half of them together, since she had decided, as she said, to go along

36

with the century. So she went. Tom Scanlon didn't. He stayed right on in Lone Tree. Lone Tree was where—the way Scanlon would put it—the century he didn't care for turned on its axis, looked up and down the tracks just the way he did, then went east. But Lone Tree, along with Tom Scanlon, stayed put.

For fifty years, closer now to sixty, he had worn a drayman's hat with brown cane sides, a license at the front, and a soft crown that shaped to his head. When he hung it on a nail, you could still see his head in it. But when they took a picture of him the week he nearly froze they wanted one without the hat, which he gave them, then he put it down somewhere and couldn't find it when they were gone. This coonskin hat he wore to please the boy. Not a hair of it was coon hair, as he told him, and the top got hot when the sun was on it, but still he wore it. Anything to please the boy.

This coat he was wearing—mohair they called it, from the horse hairs in it—was all he had left, all they would let him wear of the outfit he had worn since his wife had left him, dating from the fall Herbert Hoover had defeated a man named Smith. A brown derby pin, stamped I'M FOR AL, was there in the frayed lapel of the coat. Scanlon had not been for Al, or anybody else, but a traveling salesman known to be a Catholic had stuck the pin there and Scanlon had let it stick. The pin was part of the coat, and the coat was part of the man.

Tom Scanlon was a plainsman, but he had a seaman's creased eyes in his face. The view from his window—the one in Lone Tree, where he had the bed pulled over to the window—was every bit as wide and as empty as a view of the sea. In the early morning, with just the sky light, that was how it looked. The faded sky was like the sky at sea, the everlasting wind like the wind at sea, and the plain rolled and swelled quite a bit like the sea itself. Like the sea it was lonely, and there was no place to hide. Scanlon had never been to sea, of course, but that was beside the point.

He looked to be a man in the neighborhood of ninety, and his passing, as people referred to it, had been expected from year to year, for the last thirty years. His wife, in good health when she left him, had had that understanding with his children, and the necessary arrangements had all been made. An undertaker in Cozad, the nearest town that had one, would meet the members of the family in Seward, where they would have a simple service, then drive back to Lone Tree and bury him. His father, his mother, and such life as he had lived were buried there. But he did not die. His death was prepared, but he put it off. With little or nothing to live for, he continued to live. He had renounced his children the moment it was clear that they intended to face the future, or even worse, like his daughter Lois, make a success of it. Tom Scanlon lived—if that was the word—only in the past. When the century turned and faced the east, he stood his ground. He faced the west. He made an interesting case, as Boyd had once observed, being a man who found more to live for, in looking backward, than those who died all around him, looking ahead.

The last of nine children, his mother dying within the year she had borne him, Tom Scanlon grew up waiting on his father, who was mad as a coot. Timothy Scanlon might have been mad all of his life, but only his wife would have known that, since it was only in his later years that he talked. Bedridden, that is, he tried to talk himself out of it. He ran this hotel —that is, his wife did—and when he could no longer get up and downstairs, he crawled into the bed in the room at the back of it. The single window looked down the railroad tracks to the west. His son, Tom Scanlon, would go up with his meals, sit there on the bed while the old man ate, then listen to him talk while he smoked his daily cigar. He was an odd one. Even the boy knew that. He slept in his clothes, lying out on top of the bed. If it got cold he might throw a comfort over his feet. One reason for that might be the fact that he wore cavalry boots, with tinkling silver spurs, that he found it harder and harder to get off. The spurs were made of iron, and even rusty, but little silver drops were attached to the rowels, and when he tapped the boot on the foot of the bed they made a tinkling sound. He also wore a leather jerkin, so dirty on the front that it looked like a piece of greasy oilcloth, and on a cord from his neck was suspended a powder horn and a firing wire. Also an awl, with a cherry wood handle, a bottle he had carved from an antelope's horn, and a small piece of leather with nipples on it for caps. They were the clothes he had worn, and the things he had used, as a young man. He saw less and less reason, as he told the boy, for taking them off.

But he was not full of yarns, as people said, but just one long yarn, told over and over, so long and drawn-out that only the boy had heard the end of it. He had heard it many times. He never seemed to tire of it. The reason was his age—as his daughter pointed out— he was going on seven or eight at the time, and that same age group were Davy Crockett crazy at the present time. But her grandchild, just as crazy as the rest, would grow out of it. Her father didn't. He had been Davy Crockett crazy all his life. Nor was it hard to see why, according to his daughter, if you knew Lone Tree, where he was born. In growing up there when he did he felt no need to get out of it. *His* father had opened the West, his brothers had closed it, and his children had gone East. Everything had been done. Everything, that is, but just stay put.

If you knew Lone Tree—if you knew it, that is, right around the turn of the century, you might get an inkling as to why Tom Scanlon stayed. What was it like? A photograph had been taken of it. From a balloon, at an estimated height of two hundred thirty feet. Dated on the back July 4th, 1901. The century had just turned. The locomotive in the picture was headed East. It had come from the East—as a matter of fact, it had *backed* in from the East since there was no local roundhouse—and the balloon was due in Omaha later that night.

The town itself, the lone cottonwood tree, the row of tin-roofed buildings and the railroad tracks, seemed to dangle like toys at the far end of a string. On the roof of the hotel were the men who had gathered to watch the balloon rise. William Jennings Bryan, the man who might have been President, was one of them. Around the cottonwood tree, in its shade, were the ladies fanning themselves, and a water sprinkler that had dripped a dark trail in the dust. Down the tracks to the west, like a headless bird with the bloody neck still bleeding, the new tublike water tank sat high on stilts. A bunch of long-stemmed grass grew where the spout dripped on the tracks. To the east, beyond the new hotel, stood the lone cottonwood tree, dead at the top but with clumps of leaves near the bottom, like a man stripped for action. Out of the clumps the dead branches curved like cattle horns. The Western Hotel, a three story structure faced with sandstone blocks and red brick, sat where the caboose of the westbound trains came to a stop. The hotel faced the plain, once called a square, where a mixture of hardy grass had been planted, and it was believed that the town would appear like the orchards in the seed catalogues. A man with time on his hands, like young Tom Scanlon, could watch it grow. The picture had been taken to impress Eastern men that there was a future in Lone Tree, and a copy of it hung in the hotel lobby, with the calendars. Tom Scanlon, his shoeless feet propped on the desk top, used to sit and look at it.

Across the street stood the bank, with its marble front, a door to go in and one to come out, but turned into a movie palace before the money arrived from Omaha. In the empty lot adjoining were the rubber tired wheels of a fire hose cart, without the hose, and a strip of wooden sidewalk, like a fence blown over on its side. A city hall, to house the hose cart and the Sheriff, was planned, but never put up. At the back of the Feed Store, under the racks of harness, was the covered wagon that belonged to Tim Scanlon, in which he had traveled West, and in which five of his sons were born. Later known as the Dead Wagon, it had been used for funerals. Still later, it was used in parades in nearby towns. In the photograph it looked like a caterpillar put on wheels, to please the kiddies, and bore a legend that had been painted on both sides.

LONE TREE
The BIGGEST little town in the World

Timothy Scanlon's wife, an Ohio girl who had made the trip to California with him, had given the town, just a tree then, its name. In her opinion that was how it looked. A lonely tree in the midst of a lonely plain. Not much had changed—in so far as you could tell from the photograph.

Before the old man finally died (as of course he

did) his son, Tom Scanlon, may have thought him immortal, his mind full of his deathless deeds. Because of the timeless life the old man had lived when young, something died in them both—as the doctor put it—leaving one you could bury, and one you couldn't, but in any sense that mattered just about as dead.

But a lifetime later, almost several of them, after being as good as dead for four generations, Tom Scanlon had suddenly turned up alive. Almost. One of the brakemen on the eastbound freight—one of the few who stopped for water—had found him in the kitchen of the Western Hotel almost frozen to death. The coal fire in the kitchen range had long burned out. He had been found sitting there, his feet in the oven, wrapped up in blankets and buffalo hides, a cold cigar in his mouth as if waiting for spring. Some of the brakemen were accustomed, summer and winter, to see the glow of his cigar in the curtainless window, since he had moved to his father's old room at the rear of the hotel. Men working on the tracks, or those hired to burn the ditch grass, might see, both morning and evening, the matches he struck on the sill of the window, or the rim of his pot. He was in bed, but he usually slept in it sitting up. He claimed that it made his wheezy breathing easier. There was some truth in that, but of course the thing that made his breathing hard in the first place was the open window, and the asthma he got from the burning grass.

But he was free—as he told his children—to do as he liked. To sleep in his clothes, or to just lie there and not sleep. He owned the bed. He slept in it alone. In the summer he liked the window open, in the winter he liked it closed, but summer and winter he liked to lie there looking out. There was nothing to see, but perhaps that was what he liked about it.

But the winter he froze—that is, almost—something had to be done about it, and his youngest daughter,

Lois McKee, had the largest house; almost empty, since her own children had grown up and moved out. Those children, naturally, had seldom seen him; he was the ghost in the family closet, and there was nothing to be gained—they understood—in bringing him out. Since he put off dying it had not been necessary to bury him. He was still there, that is, when another generation made its appearance—oddly enough, at the same time he did, and in the same house. Gordon Scanlon McKee, the old man's great-grandson, wearing a coonskin hat and sporting two six-shooters, had been the first member of the family, so to speak, to speak to him. It had been love—as the family feared—at first shot.

Tom Scanlon never cared for his own children, but he hardly knew why until they grew up and had children of their own. Then he saw it. What the world had been coming to, had arrived. What could you expect of the younger generation if they had fathers like McKee, a hog shooter? Nothing. Which was pretty much what they got.

For twenty years—no, it was more like thirty—Scanlon hadn't said more than "Clippers in the back, Eddie," which he said to the barber over in Cozad about every six weeks. When the boy came along he had to learn to talk all over again. Not so much at first, since the boy did the talking, but when they got in the back seat of the car, way back where they put them, why, then he was free to talk a little more. The country they were in, which was south of El Paso, was dry and open the way his father had described it —country where there was nothing for the wind to blow on but himself. When a man died out there, which was often, they had to bury him deep, pile some big rocks on him, then run the wagons over him if they wanted to keep him dead. Otherwise the Indians or the coyotes would dig him up. Once his father saw an Indian with a hat he'd made from a wagon lantern, like a sort of helmet, the lantern door like a visor he could wear up, or down. He told the boy. The boy liked to hear stories like that. Just the telling of it led him to think of another one. One of the old squaws with a big family used to follow the wagons and live off the garbage, but the trouble was she had more little shavers than she could get on her horse. So what'd she do? Different than most squaws, she was smart. She rigged up a sort of sled, using saplings for runners, which she could trail along behind her little pony, and back on the sled, just as pretty as you please, were all her kids. Might not have been hers at all, but she'd adopted them.

The boy couldn't hear enough stories like that, and when they both got sick, on the little wild bananas, they had to sleep in the car, which got him to remembering more of them. That place where the flowers bloomed only at night, and this girl in the wagon, whose name was Samantha, kept fireflies in a bottle so when they buzzed their lanterns she could look at them. The flowers, that is. And while she looked at the flowers, Timothy Scanlon could look at her face. Well as he could see it, he couldn't tell you what it was like. He (his father, that is) said her hair was black as it was where the harness scuffed the hair off a mule's hide, but when he looked at her eyes he looked right through them without seeing anything. He couldn't tell you, he said, what color they were. All he could tell you was they weren't like his own eyes much, since she only saw different things with them—from the seat of the wagon she would see a flower, where he only saw a track. Even when she pointed and they looked at it together, they never saw the same thing.

That was something for the boy, so Scanlon told

him that; the more he talked the more he remembered, and the more he remembered the nearer all of it seemed. He couldn't see more than the light out there in the bullring, but let him close his eyes, and just remember, and he could see from the fork of the Platte to Chimney Rock. The buffalo like an island with a brown furze on it, the wind blowing, the wagons strung out in a line like so many caterpillars with their fuzz burned off.

The truth was, he didn't know he was so blind until they came for him. In Lone Tree, where nothing had changed, he saw things in their places without the need to look at them. They were there, in case he wanted to see them, in his mind's eye. All he had to do was close his eyes and look at them. That was how it was with this remembering business, and one reason he talked so much, once he got started, was that the more he talked the clearer it all became. Back around El Paso, where he began to get started, he would say, "I tell you how they shot the Mormon?" but the boy couldn't seem to get it straight through his head who he meant by *they*. He seemed to think Scanlon did it. He always said *you* when Scanlon meant *they*. Since he couldn't seem to get it straight in his head, and since it simplified the story to tell it that way, Scanlon found it easier to go along with it, and just say we. And the more he told it that way, the truer it seemed.

"I tell you how *we* put in the time?" he would say, and it seemed that he had. He had put more of it in back there than anywhere else. Anyhow, that's how it seemed. That he had put that time in, all of it, himself.

"Don't it take you back, Gordon?" he heard McKee say, a man who never once had a place to go back to, who had done nothing but try to go forward all of his life.

"I tell you how—" he began, and poked his elbow

in the boy, but blind as he was he could see the commotion, people jumping up like popcorn, and the boy hopped up like he'd sat down on a pin. But where the light was, out there in the bullring, he saw nothing, just the slope beyond it spotted with snow and scrub trees of some sort, blowing in the wind. He closed his eyes. He remembered where it was, and just how it had been.

Boyd

If you had asked Boyd who the one man was he would never live to see in Mexico, if you had wanted an answer, that is, he would have said McKee. Rather quickly, in fact, as if he had asked himself that question. Which was the case, oddly enough, since people *like* McKee, thousands of them, were crawling out of the woodwork all over Mexico. They could be found in Guanajuato, photographed in Paztcuaro, touched for a five spot in Acapulco, and observed with bowed heads in the tunnels of the bullring whooping up their lunch. Good honest corn-fed people with the hard to wrinkle suits, the new two-toned car with the *Turista* sticker, and the kid on the bumper hired to watch the hub caps and the stuff piled on the seats. Baskets from Oaxaca, blankets from Cuernavaca, gems from Querétaro and the new Sears, Roebuck, plus several of those crackling steerhide chairs that looked and sounded like musical instruments. All of them like McKee, with one exception. Only one would have Lois McKee along with him, a serene wooden Indian equally blended of fire and ice. The chaste virginal mother of three sons and nine grandchildren. All by divine compensation, miraculous birth, since husband and wife shared the ice side together. The fire side, as Boyd could tell you, had long been out. He had been the one to blow it alive, then let it go out.

"Anybody ever show you this, son?" he said, and took the boy's Pepsi bottle, gave it a shake, then let a thin spray of the liquid squirt over the rail and stain the board fence of the bullring. The boy's eyes popped. Boyd could see that nobody had showed him that one.

"How's that?" he said, shook the bottle again, and let it arch and fall on the sand in the runway. The way Boyd used to stand, after drinking pop, and pee in the soft hot dust behind the firehouse, making a sound like a quick summer shower in the road. He always drank red pop hoping he would pee red, but he never did. "How's that, boy?" he said, and arched a thin stream clear over the runway into the bullring. One of the bullfighter's *peones*, leaning on the funk hole, gazed at him with admiration.

"Let me!" said the boy, and reached for the bottle.

"Easy now," said Boyd, and kept a grip on it. He peered down the row to see if one of the McKees had been in on that. No sign. No visible sign of life, that is. Did these bones live? It hardly seemed possible. Fossils. In what was usually described as an excellent state of preservation. Where found? In the pits around a bullring. Exhibiting the usual state of high animation. What did they feel? What would they see? They would feel and see what they had brought along with them. The Passion of the Bullring as seen from the deep-freeze along the Platte. The final goring of old Bullslinger Boyd.

"Let me squirt it!" said the boy, and reached for the bottle.

Boyd took a swig of what was left and said, "It ain't what it used to be, Crockett. When I was your age we could drink it or squirt it. Think I'd just squirt it now."

That pleased the boy, but the old fool in the seat beside him said, "Hmmmmmmphhh." Only sound he had made. What passion had forced it out of him? Jealousy. His old man's lust to possess the ears and eyes of the boy. His own fading. Deaf? No, just a little *deaf*. Cloudy snot-green eyes with a cataract blur. More like a horned toad than a man, a big one, trained to grunt noises, and go around on a leash wearing an imitation coonskin hat.

"Us boys—" he said, looking the boy in the eye, the sea-born eyes in the plainsman's face, "us boys like our powder dry, and our likker straight."

"What's straight?" said the boy. In his open mouth, the flesh-pink scented wad of blowgum. At the moment sidetracked. He couldn't chew, blow *and* think.

"They tell me Davy Crockett was straight," Boyd said, and paused to wonder, rocking the Pepsi bottle. The boy aimed his plastic pistol, fired it, and sang—

> "He feared no man, he feared no beast,
> And hell itself he feared the least."

"*Hell?*" checked Boyd.

The boy nodded. He took a quick suck on the barrel of his gun, then added, "If you want to go to heaven, you got to go to hell *first*."

Mirror-like the ice-blue eyes that Boyd looked into returned his gaze. Sober.

"So you want to go to heaven?" he inquired.

"I do if I can go to hell *first*," was the reply.

Did Boyd seem to doubt that? The boy turned on his seat, poked the old man with his gun, then said, "Don't I?"

"Shortest way to heaven's right smack through hell," the old man barked.

Boyd swallowed. Over the old man's head, the plastic crown of his hat, Boyd peered down the row at the old man's daughter. Did she know *that* sort of thing was going on? That heaven, hell and God knows what else were being bandied about? She didn't seem to. Still no visible scars of life. She sat stiffly erect, laced into her corset of character. Another way to heaven, Boyd reflected, was right smack through the hell of such a woman. Had McKee made it? He sat there chewing on a match. It skipped from one corner of his mouth to the other, flicked by his tongue. A match that he had lit, then allowed to burn down so one end, as he said, was charcoal, with just enough sulphur in the head to sweeten the breath.

McKee had been doing that, believing that, for more than forty years. Picked it up as a kid and never had reason to question it. The way he picked up, the way he did not question, everything else. His life, for instance. A simple frame-house sort of life with an upstairs and a downstairs, and a kitchen where he lived, a parlor where he didn't, a stove where the children could dress on winter mornings, a porch where time could be passed summer evenings, an attic for the preservation of the past, a basement for tinkering with the future, and a bedroom for making such connections as the nature of the house would stand. In the closets principles, salted down with moth balls. In the storm-cave, sprouting like potatoes, prejudices. A good man, salt of the earth, suspicious of eggheads, but drawn to them, a practical cogitator but believer in mysteries, soberly mindless but afflicted with thinking, conscientiously unconscious, civic pillar by day, daydreamer by night.

Had such a man picked up a friend like Boyd? Had he picked such a wife? If Boyd could read and understand the signs, he had not. They had picked him. It seemed strange. What did the likes of McKee have to offer *them?* Perhaps only what they needed—if what they needed was a witness. And they did.

McKee was a believer. Having settled on something he kept the faith. The healing property of matches, the beauty of women, and the strange dreams of Boyd were all acceptable to him. He believed. He made, that is, such things possible. He also made them, alas, highly expendable. A row of ghostly light poles without lights in the grassy suburbs of his imagination, where his children, or his children's children, or their children, might live.

But not McKee. No, Walter McKee was a simple, modest man.

Mrs. McKee and me couldn't be happier.

That was what he had said. That was what he meant, so it was naturally what he had said.

"Oh, Boyd!" called McKee, catching his eye, then stopped as if he saw there what Boyd had been thinking. He turned to gaze at the bullring, the parade of matadors in their suits of light, their artificial pigtails, gliding across the sand with the slinky gait of cats that had learned to walk on their hind legs. Behind them the padded nags, with their fat-assed Sancho Panzas, the pom-pommed mules dragging their heavy chains, and then the proletariat prepared to endure it all— then clean it up. The head and tail, as Lehmann liked to say, of the bull himself. A centaur with a God emerging at the front, but all bull at the rear.

"What're the mules for?" said McKee, but Boyd had the feeling that was not the question. He let Dr. Lehmann, his lips shiny with brandy, answer it. It gave Boyd another chance to sit and stare, as if he was listening, at the woman trapped between them—the lips a skimmed milk blue, but the eyes serene as ever. *What* was on her mind? All signs and portents to the contrary, he knew a mind was there. It had, after all, once spoken to him. What had brought her to the bullfight had also brought her, thirty years before, to the edge of darkness, that twilight zone on the porch where anything might happen, and sometimes did.

Invisible zones, like the circles in a bullring that were meant to stylize and limit the action, with the light above the screen door, the funk hole of the porch, the legitimate escape. But Boyd, with a little fancy cape work, had crossed the line. No more, no gorings nor bloody linen, but a foretaste, such lineaments of pleasure that what followed, if anything should follow, would be an afterthought.

What else had brought her to the bullfight? A thirty-years-after thought? The tribal memory of a man, that is, a lover, that a woman knew better than trust. What manner of man was that? The one who took *advantage* of her. If a man would be remembered, he would give and take only that.

What a crazy goddam world, Boyd was thinking—and so made room for himself. Also for Dr. Lehmann, the celebrated quack, with nothing to recommend him but his cures, and Paula Kahler, the only sort of failure he could afford. Also for old man Scanlon, the living fossil, for McKee, the co-inventor of the dust bowl, for his wife, the deep-freeze, and her grandson who would live it all over again. Here gathered at a bullfight. The sanded navel of the world. Gazing at this fleshy button each man had the eyes to see only himself. This crisp sabbath afternoon forty thousand pairs of eyes would gaze down on forty thousand separate bullfights, seeing it all very clearly, missing only the one that was said to take place. Forty thousand latent heroes, as many gorings, so many artful dodges it beggared description, two hundred thousand bulls, horses, mules and monsters half man, half beast. In all this zoo, this bloody constellation, only two men and six bulls would be missing. Those in the bullring. Those they would see with their very own eyes. This golden eye would reflect, like a mirror, every gaze that was directed toward it—like the hub caps, Boyd

thought, displayed on their racks along the boule-
vards. Shining like medieval armor, available in all
sizes, taken in jousting at night, offered for sale in
the morning, this nickel-plated mirror was the modern
man's escutcheon. In it he saw, distorted to his own
taste, this fantasy of himself. A simple *Ford* man, a
sporty *Jag* man, an old *Stutz* man, a modern *Volks*
man, with the Family man at the wheel of the *Subur-
ban*, the door monogrammed.

Any blot on these escutcheons?

Boyd stared, as he would for dents and scratches,
from face to face. Scratches and scars could be painted
over, broken parts replaced. In the face of McKee he
could see a firm believer in Authorized Service & Parts.

"Well, folks—" he said, giving Boyd a wink, "what's
next on the bill?"

Boyd put up his right hand, wagging the Pepsi bottle, to indicate that *he* was, and he rose from the seat
having in mind a little speech. God knows what. After
he had made it, he would know. Something about old
times, escutcheons, and the strange reflections in hub
caps. Take Boyd's. It might surprise you what he saw.
But nobody heard what little he said. The horn, the
shrill blast of the trumpet, spun McKee around as
though someone had twirled him, and he stood with
his back to the ring when the bull came in.

A bull? The sound of the horn itself seemed to
frighten him. Then the ring, the empty enclosure, the
turtle-like heads of the men at the funk holes. All of
it strange and unfriendly—except for the man waving
at him. At the edge of the ring, over on the shade side,
a man who waved a Pepsi-Cola bottle, then held it out
before him and shot a spray of it into the air. Was the
little bull thirsty? *Something* about it appealed to him.
He came toward it, he ignored the shouts, the man
who came and fanned a cape at him, the one who
moved around behind and tried to get a grip on his

tail. He reached the fence, where he dragged his chin along the rough top rail, like a mooncalf, pausing for a moment to roll his black eyes at McKee.

"You thirsty, boy?" Boyd yelled, gave the bottle a shake, felt the pressure fizz around his finger, then let a stream of the liquid arch across the runway, splash on the bull's moist snout. The swollen grape-blue tongue slipped out, slapped the froth of it off.

"You like it, eh?" Boyd cried, shook the bottle again, and shot a thin seltzer stream of it into his mouth. He loved it. The tongue lobbed out, mop-wise, and wiped it off. Boyd heard the crowd roar behind him—someone shouted *ole!*—and he turned to sweep off his hat, make a bow. He kissed the frothy tips of his fingers, blew them at the crowd. They loved it, the shouting grew louder, he gave the bottle a last frenzied shake, and then, with every eye fastened on him, he turned the bottle from the bull toward himself. Was this *la suerte suprema?* Boyd's moment of truth? Perhaps. One hand upraised, for quiet, he tipped his head back, opened his mouth, and shot the last feeble squirt of the liquid down his own throat. In the thunder of applause that followed he bowed, took his seat. Just in time, since his head was whirling, he felt the clubbing thump of his heart, and as Lehmann had told him it might now, any day, he waited for it to stop.

But it didn't. Like everything else, *that* too slipped out of his grasp.

No, it didn't.

Knowing that it wouldn't, not here and now—when Boyd died it would be anticlimactic—Lehmann settled back and watched the long-horned cows come in.

Lehmann

The friendly bull, wet and sticky with pop, shooed like a stray chicken by men with capes, made a wide-eyed tour of the ring, then followed the cows. The crowd roared—as well they might, being full of friendly bulls with a weakness for cows, and cows with a weakness for such a curious bull as Boyd. A charmer. One who mastered the bull with a sharp squirt of pop.

If you began in the morning—as Lehmann once had—and followed Gordon Boyd from bar to bar, from bench to bench, from corner to corner, you would reach the conclusion that he was a lonely man. He seemed to have no friends. That was how it looked. But Lehmann had sensed something was wrong. With that picture. With that tableau of loneliness. Boyd was alone, but seldom lonely, since the empty stool was in a crowded bar, the corner at a busy intersection, and the vacant bench was along the walk in a thronging park. He sat alone amidst gossip, pigeons, children, and photogenic squirrels. He liked to be alone surrounded by others, solitary, that is, rather than lonely, since the smell of something living, rotting, or dying seemed important to him. All that he had. He had been dying for years, himself. Only his fear of muffing that, also, kept him alive.

Where had it begun? In the beginning, like everything else. One had to take the ends of a frazzled string, or the soiled threads of a flannel pocket, and follow them back, back to the heart of the labyrinth. As Lehmann had done. He had gazed into the sightless eyes of the Minotaur. Half man, half myth, the emerging God, dream-haunted, gazed toward the light with eyes in which the pupils had not been drilled. If only the impossible seemed worth doing, Boyd would end up doing nothing. Which had occurred. But he had failed at even that. The clichés of success, from which he rebelled, had taken their revenge in his passion for failure. Too late—almost too late—Boyd had discovered that the one cliché, stamped Success on one side, Failure on the other, rang hollow at both extremities.

Lehmann had watched the performance, one of his best, with fear, trembling and admiration, but he could have told you the aging charmer would survive. At the wrong time and place he always did. When Boyd dropped dead, as one day he would, and it might be there in the bullring, whoever found him would seriously question it. The blue lids of his eyes would be turned back, a pocket mirror held to his mouth. Though he was stone cold, they would go on looking in him for life. Finger the pulse, put an ear to his chest, apply injections, prayers, and artificial respiration, since it wouldn't seem right that a young man of such *promise* should die. Not this one. Whose promise was now fifty-some years old.

Dr. Leopold Lehmann resembled those shaggy men seen in the glass cages of the world's museums, depicting early man at some new milestone of his career. Building a fire, shaping a rock, scratching symbols on the walls of a cave, or making guttural sounds with some vague resemblance to human speech. This last he did, by common agreement, with appalling credibility. The sounds he made—a blend of Brooklynese,

German, and grunts, in proportions entirely his own—
seldom resembled anything else. He specialized in
openings that dissolved into thin air. "Wot I min iss
—" he would say, and then trace on the air, with a
hairy finger, a few cloudy symbols that his older patients claimed to understand. Born in Goethe's town
of Weimar, the fourth son of a cheese importer, he
had early mastered English, only to learn that it did
not pay. Broken, rather than proper, English spoke
to the soul. A battered language, like an armless sta-
tue, had more value on the market, and Dr. Lehmann
had broken, battered and glued together a language
all his own.

"Thod iss olter"—he would say, to everyone's joy—
"than Atom und efenink."

It was hardly necessary to go into his background.
It was all there at the front. Vienna he knew like the
palm of the hand that was melon colored, the fingers
bent backwards, with Kärntnerstrasse, where he had
lived, rising from the pink hollow to the knuckle.
Freud he remembered: a small military man with a
dark beard, money problems, and a walk that made
Lehmann want to sneak up behind and stick a cane
between his legs.

So much for background. Foreground reflected his
varied life in America. A period of adjustment (thirty-
eight years in Brooklyn), several years of travel (from
Avenue J, via the Bridge, to Manhattan) and professional achievement (four hundred dollars in night
school awards from a package deal involving magazine
subscriptions). Dr. Lehmann was so plainly the old
world type, with pronounced Neanderthal connections, that the only question was how long he had been
in the States. "Nod lonk enuff!" he would reply,
which was true in many practical matters, and gave
the impression he was one of the well-adjusted refugee

types. This impression was correct. He had other people's problems, but few of his own.

Professionally speaking, Dr. Lehmann specialized in mental cases, usually female, that his more successful colleagues had given up. The transfer type, looking for an object that would come down with the same infection, found Dr. Lehmann sympathetic but baffling. Talent, of Dr. Lehmann's sort, was highly unorthodox. At a point in the treatment, usually without warning, he would clamp on his huge head a pair of earphones, which transformed him, in a twinkling, into a Flying Saucer pilot, or a Space Cadet. A psychological trick? A sort of Rorschach test? No, Dr. Lehmann was a lover of music, the quartets of Haydn and Mozart in particular. If a female patient, at the sight of Dr. Lehmann, remote as early man behind his earphones—if this patient, say, should raise her voice, do anything unduly to crack through the barrier, Dr. Lehmann would raise a hairy finger, wag it, then hiss softly, "Moww-Tzzzzzzarrrrt isss spikink." That left up to the patient the question of priority. Few felt up to the challenge. Those who did soon went somewhere else. Dr. Lehmann took pains to make it clear, at the outset, that he knew nothing of the body, little of the mind, but that he had an arrangement of sorts with the soul. The odd thing was that he seemed to. No, the odd thing was that he did.

His *im*patients—as he called those who interrupted Mozart—were seldom around long enough to take the acid test. A little fable, hardly more, told by Dr. Lehmann those summer evenings when nothing at all seemed to be seriously wrong with the world. During his *drainink*, as he called it, he had lived in Vienna with a Frau Klinger, a woman from Buda-Pest, who had one son. A frail, pasty-faced young man named Karl, he would bring Dr. Lehmann his *schokolade* in the morning, along with a machine that made something Karl Klinger called a cigarette. It stuffed something like moss into paper tubes that could be smoked. That was of no importance to the story—just an aside of the sort that Dr. Lehmann, when he talked about *anything*, was more or less inclined to make. He and young Klinger often smoked a paper tube together, that is. The days were gray in Vienna, a city of old people, and for Christmas Dr. Lehmann went to Venice, which was no place to go, but that was what he did. No more than four or five days. But on his return Karl Klinger was gone. In less than a week he had taken sick and died. Frau Klinger passed on to Dr. Lehmann his cigarette machine.

One day in the spring—Dr. Lehmann remembered it had been very balmy, and the windows were open—he had been at work, as usual, in the dissecting room. Although the windows were open, the air was strong with formaldehyde. From the basket on the floor, full of hands and feet—they were not at all squeamish in Vienna—he had selected the pale, blue-veined hand of a child. Or a young girl. That was how it looked. Not until he had placed it on the table did he notice the nicotine stain on the fingers, and the way all of the nails were chewed. Karl Klinger, as he meant to say, chewed on his nails all the time.

That was the story. Dr. Leopold Lehmann would tell it casually. In the silence that followed he would sip his brandy, a stimulant to his poor circulation, and the shiny valspar film would remain on his lips.

What did it mean? What did *he* mean, that is? On the slightest pretext he would bring up the story—but always *up*, never down to something like brass tacks, concrete statements, or simple answers to direct questions.

Such as—was it fiction, this fable, or was it fact? Was Karl Klinger real—God forbid—or the front for somebody else, a necessary fiction that professional ethics—or was it esthetics—made imperative? There were those who intimated that the case of Paula Kahler—if she was a *case*—would throw the missing light on Karl Klinger's remains. But just try and pin the storyteller down. On his head would go the earphones, on his face the stone-age smile of early man.

Some patients, understandably, found it too much of a strain. Others, for various reasons, found it somewhat gruesome but interesting. So Lehmann had two kinds of clients. Those who left. And those who stayed. If the patient could put up with that sort of thing, Dr. Lehmann could put up with the patient. Gordon Boyd was one—he had been a Lehmann man from the word no, as he put it—and Paula Kahler was another, a Lehmann man, as it turned out, in spite of herself. She was not so much his patient, as he often hinted, as his practice.

Gordon Boyd had come to Lehmann—he had not made an appointment, or appeared with the usual recommendation, but came in with the trash man and rang the service bell in the hall. Lehmann had recognized the type. The professional soldier of failure, waging the cold war within himself. A man in his forties, theatrically shabby, the boyish face still resisting what his will encouraged, a deterioration that was meant to be total and picturesque. In the pocket of his raincoat—dropping to the floor when he fumbled for some matches—he had a piece of flannel cloth, soiled and grass stained, that Lehmann took to be a sort of shoe rag. He did not inquire about it. Boyd, without comment, had returned it to his coat. But later, as he was leaving, Boyd slipped the rag from his pocket and held it up as if the pattern would show in the light.

"For apful polishink?" Lehmann had suggested.

"Ty Cobb's pocket," Boyd had said, matter-of-factly, then added, "little Gordon Boyd's piece of the

Cross," and smiled his untouched boyish smile. Likable. Lehmann himself had suggested that he should come back. Bringing with him his pocket, the portable raft on which he floated, anchored to his childhood, on the glassy surface of the sandpit where he had failed to walk. Something of a hero, something of a madman, something of an ass.

And so he had come back—not with the pocket, that did not reappear until later—but with a photograph he had torn from some camera magazine. The photograph showed a bum, seated on a park bench, sharing his last crust of bread with a squirrel. Lehmann had smiled. He smiled at all pictures of cats, dogs, birds and squirrels. But Boyd had not smiled, which led Lehmann to feel that perhaps he had overlooked something—which he had. The bum on the bench was Boyd himself. But one wouldn't have guessed it. It seemed immaterial that the bum was Boyd.

A dedicated no-man, one who had turned to failure as a field that offered real opportunity for success, Boyd had come to Lehmann when it was clear that he had failed to fail. That he had failed to touch the floating bottom within himself. Having run the full gamut of success-clichés—including the quick rise and fall from favor—he had found Failure a nut that refused to crack. Not that he hadn't worked at it. He had given it the best years of his life. At one point he had achieved—he had believed he had achieved—the recognition he had worked for, since charitable tourists would tip him generously when they snapped his photograph. Then one day he had found, stumbled on it, as he said, in a magazine left in a trash bin, this shot of a bum feeding the squirrel in Washington Square. That had done it. His bottom had been the reverse of his top.

The camera had caught every memorable cliché: the coat fastened with a pin, the cut suggesting better days, the sock there to call attention to the calloused heel, in one soiled hand a paper bag, now empty, and in the other a crust. This crust he shared—the autumn sun shining on it—with his sole companion, a moth-eaten squirrel who had plainly suffered the same misfortunes at the hands of *life*. The clichés told the story. The face of the bum bore witness to it. But of the man behind the face, the failure behind the man, there was no evidence. Every piece of his Fall had been borrowed from the wings, from the costume rack. Of Boyd the walker-on-water, the pocket snatcher, the man who had set out to master his failure—of this man there was no inkling. For that, one had to look at the squirrel. Having been cheated by Boyd, on occasion looted, having been baited, petted and deliberately tortured, he fastened on the hand that fed him a cynical, skeptical eye. But that was not in the picture. He posed with his back to the camera.

Something of a wonder-boy in the theater, Boyd had begun with a sponsor, an empty stage, and the conviction that it should be emptier. Characters—the few he had at the beginning—became a cast of disembodied voices, speaking with the hollow accents of train loudspeakers, or apartment speaking tubes. This observation was his own. He had made a career of observing himself. But even there he had failed, as Lehmann had ironically pointed out. It was the top, not the bottom, to which he had stuck. His boyish walk on the water had not been a failure, but his first success.

In a prologue to a play that was never produced, Boyd advised his public that he *hoped* to fail, since there was no longer anything of interest to be gained in success. He went on to speak of culture as a series of acceptable clichés. A photographer's salon where ready-made frames, hung on the walls of rustically historical gardens, lacked only the faces of succeeding generations in the ready-made holes. This hand-me-down world defined the realm of the possible. The impossible—become a cliché itself—had been ruled out. This left the artist—Boyd himself, that is—with only one suitable subject, and life itself with only one ironic result. This was Failure. Such as Boyd, from the beginning, had practiced himself.

Lehmann had seen, without being told, that Boyd had thrown himself into his subject. In his failure, at least, he would be a success. He had worked at being down and out in Paris, combed the beaches and the tourists of the Riviera, and in the palmy days of fascism earned his bed and board as a rabble rouser. All of it apprentice work, an author's slumming, a Bernarr Macfadden tour to end of the night, in preparation for the pay-off, the real McCoy, when the native returned to New York and the Automat. These were the years he had sounded for the bottom off Bleecker Street. His standards had been high. Too high, perhaps. The cliché of failure, like that of success, hung on the walls of the room he decayed in, and through the hole in the ready-made frame he popped his own head. The man that McKee—Boyd had described the scene for Lehmann—had found in his B.V.D.'s in a loft in New York. Squirrel-feeder and hoarder of crusty clichés. Neither going to pot, throwing in the sponge, or even working at it had brought him failure. How achieve it? It had to be imagined, like everything else. It had to undergo a sea change, a transformation, that would indicate that failure had *happened*—as the squirrel knew—to the man behind the front. The armor of clichés kept him from touching bottom, or from being touched.

And as for *the* bottom—when Boyd had brought it up Lehmann had left the room, returned with Paula Kahler. She had been there. She had succeeded where Gordon Boyd had failed. The bottom was a long way down—as it was also a long way up. He had let Boyd, a good observer, judge the facts for himself. In time—it had taken time, since Paula Kahler had exhausted the subject—Boyd began to see there might be something in it for himself. Not in the realm of failure, this time, but success. The words that Paula Kahler had made into flesh—the words, that is, and the music—called for a further transformation, back into words again. Lehmann had made the suggestion. Boyd had taken it up. To make a beginning he had come with them to Mexico. It would make quite a story. One that Paula Kahler would never tell herself.

Could he be sure of that? Lehmann felt sure enough. Paula Kahler had learned, among other things, to do without speech. Birdlike, so fragile she looked brittle, Paula Kahler had the large sad eyes of a goat, the feet of a man, and hands unrelated to the other parts. The hands for instance, seemed to lead a life of their own. They knitted, or lay quiet in her lap like birds with their heads concealed. She had an aura, an air of peace about her, usually associated with genius or the simple-minded. The observation had been made by Dr. Lehmann, and he let it stand. There had been no need to expand upon it. Paula Kahler was enough.

For the music, shortly after the war, Dr. Lehmann would spend the summer in Salzburg, but that was before he discovered Mexico. In a newsreel theater on Fulton Street he saw a man fight a bull. The bull won. He stayed in his seat and saw it happen many times. The image of the man as part of the bull—a trick, you might say, of the camera—became fixed, like a poster, in his mind. He looked into the subject. Found where it was that men still fought bulls. It was done many places, if he could believe it, but nearest at hand was Mexico, where his friend Gordon Boyd could drive them in his car. It had been a revelation. One day he hoped to know of what.

An old man's witless passion for the life of action and romance? No, the passion was elsewhere. A passion to generalize. Never had Lehmann seen, in such small compass, so much basis for inexhaustible generalization. Man and bull. Man into bull. Bull into man. Sometimes he sat up high, for a God's perspective, up from where the huge bull looked like a BB, the object being to tip the ring and roll it into one of the funk holes. But as a rule he sat close, repelled and attracted, like the early man he so closely resembled, crouched on a rocky slope to watch a colleague battle with dinosaurs. He wore no hat, his sun tanned pate (the only hairless patch of his body) shining above the tree line from the nervous swipes he made with his mittened hand. In his pocket was an oilskin *Regenhut* in case it rained. In the *Hut*, the chin straps dangling, his natural jaundice color a shade sun darkened, he proved beyond a shadow of a doubt the great antiquity of Mexico. At his side, for professional reasons, the white-haired old lady with the lap of knitting, and the big American who often sat there reading the newspapers.

"Varm enuff?" asked Lehmann, and took the knobby hands of Paula Kahler, the knuckles bluish, and rubbed the fingers between his mittens like so many clothespins. Whose hands were they? The question naturally came to mind. Such hands on such a fragile creature, that is. Close companions to the feet, with the large corns, laced into shoes of kid leather—the shoes dating from an era when nothing above the tops was seen.

Over her lap, tucked about her sharp knees, Lehmann spread the blanket that they shared between them, the label of a Brooklyn hotel still attached to one corner of it. The Regent Arms. Dating, that is, from Lehmann's early life and interesting times. Times that had brought him, along with his language, the strange case of Paula Kahler, the chambermaid who had strangled the amorous bellhop in the servants' lift. The bellhop, an old hand at the practice, had stopped the lift between the fourth and fifth floors, and there it had stayed until the next morning, when it was missed. Paula Kahler had been found, in her aura of peace, seated on the pile of sheets she had meant to deliver, the body of the bellhop neatly covered with one of them. She had been a little bruised, physically, but psychologically undisturbed. Using nothing but the hands that did not go with the body, she had protected herself, strangled her assailant, then respectfully covered his remains with a clean sheet. When she was turned over to Dr. Lehmann, the house physician, for a routine checkup and examination, it was found that Mrs. Kahler, as she was known, was not a *Mrs.* at all. She was a man, physically normal in every respect. Nor did she at all resist the examination—in her own eyes, and what eyes they were, there was no disparity between the body she had and the clothes she took off. She was, and she remained, Paula Kahler, chambermaid. Neither mirrors, questions, nor obvious facts seemed to trouble her. Rather than make matters worse, she had been allowed to put the wrong clothes back on.

For observation—as they put it—Paula Kahler was turned over to Dr. Lehmann, since he showed more than the usual interest in her case. She moved to the spare room at the back of his apartment, made his bed, kept the place in order, and tolerated such observations as he felt obliged to make. For several months, for a year or two, Lehmann had kept a file of notes, analyzed her few comments, and waited, patiently, for the clue to out. It would be the making of Leopold Lehmann, professionally. It would be of service to the troubled world, generally.

Didn't it out? Yes, one day it slipped out. The tum-

blers fell into place and the door swung open—just
like that. So he went in? Better to say he just looked,
rather than went in. One of those views—they use
them in the movies—showing a narrow corridor, then
a door, and as that door slowly opens you—well, you
can do one of two things. You can look, you can go
in, or you can turn away. Like the blind monkey?
That was very much how Lehmann looked. But no—
or rather yes and no—since it was not that he refused
to see, but that these doors, these echoing corridors,
would go on endlessly. What there was to see, he had
seen. He came back to that. A man who believed he
was a woman. What did he make of it? What he
made of it, put very simply, was what he saw everywhere he looked, but he saw it clearer in the bullring
than anywhere else. What did he see? A transformation. He saw it take place. Before his eyes, the commonplace miracle of everyday life. You can begin with
a will, a way, and you end up with something else.
The human thing to do was to transform something,
especially yourself.

To Mrs. McKee, one of those women whose arms
seemed too long from the shoulder to the elbow,
Lehmann leaned forward to explain about the cows.
A law of nature? He smiled. The male coming to
heel when the female came in sight. Something that
Mrs. McKee, according to Boyd, really knew something about. He watched her eyes: the focus set, as
it was in Lehmann's box camera, so that all the ob-
jects in the picture were relatively sharp. Or blurred.
The selection was the work of another department.
A hopper into which everything was thrown, but
little came out.

The horn—Lehmann did not hear it where he heard
Mozart, or even voices, but rather he *felt* it, like the
scrape of a nail file or eggshell between his teeth. He
prepared to say as much—it was the sort of remark that

made sense to a woman—when he saw her eyes, the pleated curtain of the iris, open and close in the manner of a flytrap, as if that was where *she* felt such a trumpet blast. Then he turned—Paula Kahler's hand, lying on his sleeve, had lifted—and he saw the bull, fawn colored, his hump dark as the ring sand where it was shaded—he saw him come in at full gallop and where a cape hung on the fence, he went over it. The rail along the seats behind it, on the far side of the runway, splintered with the sound of ice cracking, and the big bull seemed to hang, weightless as a cave drawing, in the echo of the sound. Then he dropped from sight, noiselessly, wind-borne on the gasp of the crowd.

"Don't it take you back, Gordon?" he said, since it sure took McKee back, that sort of ruckus, to the crazy ball game where Boyd had torn the pocket off that big fellow's pants. Moment he saw them all hopping the fence like kids, he thought of that. The bull cleaning out that runway like a snowplow, going all the way around it before they caught him, then when they got him in the ring, they all had to leap-frog out again. Funny as hell. But all of it over too soon. The crazy business at the ball game was different in that respect. Game ended right there. Nothing for people to do but get up and go home.

Which they did. In spite of the fact that Gordon, right at that point, wasn't with them, since he was one of about five or six hundred kids milling around on the field. But Mr. Crete had said if he was old enough to start a ruckus like that, in a League ball game, he was very likely old enough to find his way home. Which he was. If Mr. Crete had known him better he wouldn't have brought up the point.

"Don't take you back, does it?" said McKee, but either he was getting hard of hearing, or he didn't want to be taken back. That was probably it. If McKee had been fool enough to have done it he probably wouldn't want to remember it either, since nothing any good at all had come out of it. He got himself all banged up in the commotion, dropped the foul ball he'd run out with, and come off with nothing better than the smelly pocket of this ball-player's

69

pants which he hung out. Every single other thing
in his life he'd dropped. But he still had that fool
pocket—McKee could hardly believe it, and it had
been just pitiful to see him—the last time McKee had
seen him in New York. A grown man. Nearly forty
at the time, and slipping fast.

"Remind you of anything, Lois?" he asked, although she hadn't been there, not at the ball game, but
at one time or another he had told her everything
that had happened to Boyd. Except the New York
business. He hadn't told her that. He and the boy, his
son, Gordon, that is, had gone back to see the Fair
with Roy and Agnes, the summer Mrs. McKee took
the younger children to Estes Park. In one of those
doughnut shops around Times Square Agnes had
snooped around and found Boyd's name in the phone
book, since she had never got over that case she had
on Boyd. Like a regular hick from the country she
stepped in and called him up. It was one of those dial
phones, new to her at the time, so she got her nickel
back when she tried to work it, but she stuck her
gum behind her ear and the second time around it
worked. They all heard it ring, since she had left the
door open, and when he answered she said, "Gordon,
this is Agnes," which naturally took a little while to
penetrate. He was never good on names, and he
hadn't seen her in fifteen years. But it was him, the
Boyd they knew, since whatever he answered it made
her blush, and then she opened the door and said, "He
says we should all come up."

"Where's up?" Roy had said, and Boyd told her it
was hardly anything by taxi. What he didn't tell her
was there were hardly any taxis at that time of night.
They were either full, or they didn't know how to
make them stop. It took them fifteen, twenty minutes
to find one, then another ten or twenty minutes to

get there, but McKee had no idea where it was. The street was dark as a tunnel where the driver let them out. It wasn't at all what Agnes had expected and they had to scratch matches to find the right number, since the hallway of the building he was in was dark. Then they looked high and low for an elevator, since he was up on the fifth, but they didn't find it either, so Roy suggested they walk. Up on the second floor, like a firefly in a bottle, was a light pointing out the fire escape, then no lights at all, just nothing, till they got to the top. He was standing there without his shirt in his pants and B.V.D.'s, just waiting for them. It had crossed McKee's mind it would have been just like him to have turned the lights out. What little he had on wasn't any too clean and he was changed so much McKee hardly knew him, stooped at the top, with one of those little pots that stick out in front. Agnes had been so shocked she just stood there, the way a woman will. McKee had been dumbfounded, but you could bank on Roy, who had looked all around him then said—"This is a nice little place you got here, Gordon," and it broke the ice. Not that they died laughing at it, but it broke the ice.

McKee had taken the boy by the arm and said, "You probably don't remember this little fella—" since the boy, right at that point, was taller than Boyd. A big strapping youngster the way Boyd had once been himself. Boyd had shaken his hand, then they had stepped inside into what was like a barn on top of a building. Just a big barn without hay in it. Just an empty loft. He had a bed in it, one of those cots he could cover with something and sit on later, then he had this stool, the seat cracked, that he'd been sitting on. No back to it. One it once had was broken off. Then he had this basin back in one corner, and way back, out of the light, was this toilet that McKee couldn't see, but he could hear it drip. They got to know about that since Roy had first asked him if he had the facilities handy, and McKee and Roy had gone back to use them, pulled on the light. There had been hairpins on the floor and a pair of silk stockings around the doorknob. It had been such a shock that McKee had acted as if he hadn't seen it, Roy had done the same, and that was how they both felt. Then they'd walked back into the light where he had these card tables, side by side, with a typewriter on one, and on the other one a coffee pot. Beside the coffee pot was this dirty piece of cloth, like a pot holder. While they'd been out in back Agnes must have noticed that piece of cloth, and kidded him about it, since the first thing she did was hold it up for them all to see.

"Walter—" she said, to McKee, "you know what this is?"

"Looks like a pot holder to me," he had said, to get around the fact he thought it pretty dirty.

She held it closer to the light as if she thought that might help him.

"He says you're the one person in the world who could vouch for it. What it is."

McKee had tried to think. Boyd had pulled his leg so many different ways, over the years, he couldn't think how he meant to pull it with this dirty rag.

"Guess I could vouch it's pretty dirty, all right," he had said, but nobody laughed. That was not the answer. His own boy stared at him like he knew very well he was holding something back.

"You give up then?" she said. He nodded that he gave up. "He says it's Ty Cobb's pocket," she went on. "He says you were there and saw him snatch it."

"Holy smoke!" McKee had said, something he hadn't said in years. He looked around at them all, Boyd included, then he looked back at the pocket.

It had about the right shape. He could make out the grass stains on one corner of it. He had never before set eyes on that pocket—once it had been torn from the pants—since the ruckus on the ball field had kept him from seeing what had happened to it.

"McKee—" Agnes had said—she always called him McKee when she knew she had him, and wanted an answer—"McKee, would you say this was it?"

He hadn't answered for a moment. Not that he doubted that it was, but he had his doubts about what it was she wanted. She was looking at him like a good deal more than just the pocket was in question. So was the boy.

"I would say it had the markings," McKee had said, which seemed to be about all she wanted, since she put the pocket back on the table with the coffee pot. All this time Boyd himself hadn't said anything. He had just stood there, the way they all did, and the way the dirty light bulb had been hanging McKee could see the rumpled hair on his head, but not his face. He'd let his hair grow out long, but it was thin on the top. He wore it that way, McKee could see, to cover up the thin spot.

"Ask him what he's doing with it," Agnes said, when she saw that McKee lacked the nerve to.

"I'm putting it in a book," said Boyd. "Something new in books. Small limited edition. Each book will have a piece of Ty Cobb's pocket—and Gordon Boyd's ass."

McKee had not flinched. He had expected the worst, and that was it. As Mrs. McKee had said from the beginning, he might do anything, and now he had done it. McKee had glanced at the boy, who was staring at his feet, and to show the boy how it was he should take that—

"Gordon, what you going to call this book?" he had said.

"*Touch Bottom*," Boyd had said. "The long-awaited sequel to *The Walk on the Water*."

Then they all just stood there, as though the lights had flickered, until the boy turned and bolted through the door like a kid. They could hear him on the stairs, going down two, three steps at a time. Agnes ran out in the hall and called him, but of course he didn't answer. The whole building shook a little when he got to the bottom and slammed the door.

"Well—" Boyd had said, "I guess *that* does it." But not to McKee or Roy. Nor did he say it to Agnes. He just said it, as if in passing, to himself. But women being the way they are Agnes had said—

"You guess it does *what?* You mean he won't walk on water?"

McKee had turned to look at him. The yellow light was on his hair, then down on his paunch, where his pants were unbuttoned, and he had this old clamp-style silver buckle on his belt. It wasn't even his own buckle. McKee could see it had an O, instead of a B, for the initial. They all watched him shake his head to indicate that wasn't what he meant.

"Then what do you mean?" Agnes had said, since she was a regular bulldog once she got worked up. But Boyd just stood there as if he was wondering what he meant himself. Then he seemed to remember and said—

"I guess I mean that when he touches—he won't stick."

The shooting pain—she always managed to grip him where he got this shooting pain, like something had bit him—made McKee jump as if he'd been tapped at that spot on his knee. He looked up and saw this boy —tall for a boy, but like Boyd at that age, awkward and gangly—he saw this boy walking along the back of the seats. Not with anything to sell, just walking, with people making way for him, till he got down to the rail where he swung his long legs over, then dropped. Before McKee could think what he might be up to, there he was again, climbing the ring fence, as if he didn't know what side of it the bull was on. And then, as McKee knew he would, he caught his heel on the top and sprawled on his face, making such a commotion that even the bull turned to look at him. It wasn't until then, because he dropped it, McKee noticed this stick he was holding, with a red rag about the size of a handkerchief tied to it. He scrambled for that rag like it was worth a lot of money, got his hands on it, shook the sand off, but instead of scramming for the fence he just stood there, like he was froze stiff. As well he might, since the bull had his eye on him. The bull was clean across the ring, where it was shady, but he could see the boy's white shirt in the sun, the little rag on the stick, and the way the boy's wobbly knees were locked. Otherwise his legs would have run way with him. McKee could see that, then he saw this bull, his head down so low just his horns stuck out, make a beeline for that boy, who just stood there. He didn't make a sound. He didn't move so much as a hair. He was froze in every part of his body, and when the bull hit him, right between the horns, he went up like a scarecrow that had been pitchforked into the air. Down he came, landing a little sidewise, then he crawled around like a fool bug, one with its head off, as if he had dropped something. What did that boy want? That fool stick with the rag on the end. Moment he found it he just lay flat, like he'd died on the spot.

In the meantime that bull—he'd gone by so fast it took him two, three seconds to wheel around—came back and nuzzled the boy like a hog. He tried to hook him, but it wasn't easy with him flat like that. All McKee could see was the rear of the bull, his tail like a piece of rope that was twisted, and in his own mind that boy was good as dead. He had to make up his mind if he was going to sit there and look on at it. If the boy was dead he wouldn't feel it so much, and that would be that. Then one of these men got the bull by the tail—he had this big wad at the end to hang on to—and when he swung around two of the others got in and picked the boy up. Like *they* thought he was dead, the way they dragged him— one had an arm with that stick he was holding—but what did that boy do, the moment they raised him, but stand up and walk. Not too well, a little off to one side like he thought the ring was tipped on him, and no bend at the knees at all as if he was on stilts. But walk he did, and people just moaned to see him alive, after what had happened, and in the next breath were so mad they would have liked to have seen him dead. They brought him in through the funk hole, right there below them, where McKee could see the sand stuck to his face, and a little froth of bubbles, like beer foam, around his mouth. In a way he looked more dead than alive—as if he *knew* he was dead, and had to unlearn it—but there was not a hole in him except for this tiny red spot on his shirt. Seeing nothing more than that scratch on him almost made McKee mad. The palms of his own hands were so wet he had to wipe them on his knees to dry them, and aloud he said "Too dam bad it didn't kill him," but not really meaning it. Then he waited for Mrs. McKee to ask him what in heaven's name he meant by *that*—but she didn't. Nor did her hand lift from his arm. He put his own on it—that is, he just touched to indicate he *knew* what she was thinking—but when she didn't draw the hand to her lap, he glanced at her.

"The boor chile!" Dr. Lehmann said, and there was Mrs. McKee's head lolling on his shoulder, her mouth open, and the gold caps of her teeth catching the light. "The boor chile!" Dr. Lehmann repeated, and into her mouth, from the flask he was holding, he let the drops of the brandy, honey colored, drip on her teeth and lips.

McKee sat there. It was something new in his life.

"She hass pass oud!" Dr. Lehmann said and smiled like a man christening a baby.

Wetting his lips, McKee recovered the power of speech.

"She's sure passed out, all right," he said, "or you'd never get away with something like that."

He turned to smile at the smiling, good-humored, sympathetic row of Mexicans. Two were already standing, fanning her face with their big straw hats.

Mrs. McKee

"Lois," he said, "you all right?" Cool air stirred the hair on her forehead, and feeling the chill on her face and throat she opened her eyes to face the flutter of fanning straw hats. Behind the hats, beaming with humor and concern, their heads like mops scented with hair oil, four or five Indians hovered over her like strange birds. As he waved his hat, absently, one of them ate a banana, fanning her with the sweet odor.

Had he been yelling? Was he faint himself? She wouldn't have recognized him by his voice, but only McKee, at such a time, would have called her *Lois*. Not honey, hardly ever dear, in more than forty years she had once been darling, but that was on a postcard he had mailed to her from New York. He was not a man to show his emotions, if that was what he felt.

"Tell them to stop it, will you?" she said, since she was almost freezing in some places, but felt damp all over beneath her clothes.

"Boys—" McKee began, as if they understood that, but Dr. Lehmann said something in Spanish, wagged his hand back and forth, and they stopped. But they went on staring. Did they come here for the bull, or to see a woman faint?

"Tell them—" she began, then she stopped, tasting for the first time the flavor on her lips, the coolness in her mouth as if she had swallowed some Vaporub.

"A cup of coffee," said McKee, "and you'll never know what hit you."

But she did. If she never knew anything else, she knew that. After what had happened to her on the pyramid she not only knew, she had the words for it. Oxygen hunger. Due to the altitude? "Well, I've been higher in my time," she said, when the Mexican doctor asked her, and being one of those Latins he had just stood there and looked at her.

The highest point in her life, as Alice Morple could have told him, was on the front porch of her home in Lincoln, where the altitude was nil, but the symptoms were the same. Queasiness, duck bumps, and that folding chair feeling in her elbows and knees. She knew *exactly* what had hit her, and it *wasn't* the bull that had hit that poor boy. She knew not only what had hit her, but where, and when that crazy boy went over the fence, she hadn't fainted at all, strictly speaking, she had *swooned*. Hadn't Alice Morple warned her that one day her dream would come true? "*That* type of boy," she had said, moistening her lips, "just loves to go over your fence."

"Let's go get you that cup of Java," said McKee, which was the way he talked when he needed it himself, and the only way to keep from hearing more of it was to go along. She thanked Dr. Lehmann—she could also thank the Lord that *he* had been in that seat, and not Boyd—then she got to her feet. She could *leave* anything, what killed her was to *go*. In that hoarse whisper that attracted more attention than if he had shouted, McKee said, "I'll put her in the car. Got a heater in it. You wanna keep an eye on this seat for me?"

His *seat*. Not his grandson. He would leave the child in the strangest places, and ask a perfect stranger to keep an eye on him. She had found him in the supermarket with a woman who had four of her own. McKee had left the boy to watch the market cart, and then asked the woman to watch the boy. Around the aisle, the only surface anywhere that didn't slope up or down, or seem to, she headed for the tunnel where she had come in. She did not glance back. Like a cat, if she had got in, she knew her way out. Coming up behind her, never beside her, always that tag-along step behind her, she could hear McKee walking on the cuffs of his new pants.

"Makes you think of old times, don't it?" he said, and she actually turned, thinking she would see Boyd waving at them, squirting pop or something, since what other old times were there? But that wasn't what he meant. He stood with his eyes closed, inhaling deeply, the old times that he meant being the smell of manure blowing toward them on the tunnel draft. "Guess that's one thing about bulls," he said, "that doesn't change much."

Did anything really? Take McKee. Did he ever make her think of anything but *old* times. And Boyd, standing up in that seat to squirt Pepsi-Cola into the bull's face—the same look on his face, if she could believe her eyes, that he had had on the porch. Not the same face, no, that did change, but not the look behind it, the eyes shining from the porch light where the big June bugs were trapped. *That* made her think of old times, it made her wonder, that is, if anything in the world had really happened since McKee's best friend had kissed the girl he hadn't kissed himself. McKee looking on with that silly absent-minded smile on his face. Being *reminded*, as it turned out later, of something else at the very moment an absolute stranger had pressed his lips to *her* lips. And the girl who was kissed? She hadn't changed much either now that she knew what had hit her. Knowing what had hit her, and where, she had swooned.

Was she—as Alice Morple had said—drunk on Jove's nectar like the girl in the play, and were they still, all of them, back on the porch with the creaking swing? Her Aunt Agnes, a woman in her thirties, acting skittish as a girl the moment she saw him, giggling into her apron, then excusing herself to go powder her face, put on black silk stockings, and rinse off the very plates she had asked the boys to help them do. She had also scrounged around and found one of those aprons she gave people for Christmas, and never thought of wearing, and slipped the bib over Gordon's head herself. Standing right before him, her heels out of her shoes since she had to stretch to do it, putting the loop around his neck the way only his mother should. Alice Morple herself, who just hated the kitchen, and had worn her best dress for no other reason, had been perfectly happy with a rag around her middle, washing anything. Five of them, that is, in this narrow kitchen where Agnes complained if there were more than two people, and they took three hours to do dishes she could do herself in twenty minutes. Just four really, since Agnes laughed so hard at everything he said she wasn't really useful, and spent most of the time lying on the sofa showing her pretty legs. Agnes hardly knew—as she kept saying—if she would have the strength to play pinochle, but when the dishes were done her strength suddenly returned. Instead of going to a movie, as she had first planned, she came back with popcorn balls and candied apples, and persuaded them all to play with her new Ouija board. The board didn't spell out anything useful, but pointed at *her* whenever Boyd's fingers touched it, and Alice Morple hadn't been so distracted she hadn't noticed *that*. Eating the apple, Alice Morple pretended it would turn on the stick unless Boyd was there to hold it, which he could only do, sticky and slippery as it was, by using his teeth. Then she would take such a gulp that their noses just had to touch. When they had run out of apples and marshmallows they went into the kitchen and made divinity fudge, but after all they had eaten nobody could touch any of it. *That* was what did it—when she had time to think she could see that perhaps more dishes, or even candied apples—but after candied apples you can't eat something like divinity fudge. They didn't, and the next thing she knew they were out on the porch. Alone out there, since her Aunt Agnes had excused herself, at that point, and run upstairs to the room at the front of the house. If there was a moment Alice Morple *wasn't* giggling, she would know about it. But there wasn't, so far as she knew, until he was there, smiling right above her, and the next thing she knew was the taste of candied apples on her lips. And then Alice Morple—her neck out like a goose, the pigeon bust she was so proud of out like a bumper—kissed him such a smack that her Aunt Agnes turned the bathroom water on. Strange to say, she could *not* believe her eyes, but she could believe her ears. Then he went off—it didn't cross her mind that *they* went off, both Boyd and Walter, and that Walter McKee, her fiancé, had not kissed her himself. *That* would have shocked her. Which was naturally why he had never thought of doing it.

"See here, Lois?" he said, wagging his hand at her, then pointing with it at something behind the fence. "Here in the pen they look friendly. Friendlier than that hog I was telling you about."

What it meant was they were still all out on that porch. Alice Morple had sent her clippings, for years, every time she saw him mentioned in an Omaha paper, and when he stopped being mentioned she would write and ask if there was any *news*. They both knew, without her saying so, just what she meant. It wasn't only her father who was trapped in the past, who didn't turn with the century as her mother described it, but also all of the people who had once been young, with dishes to wipe. And after wiping the dishes had stepped, for just a moment, out on the porch. Trapped. If she could believe her eyes, Boyd was trapped there himself.

For what other reason had he asked them to a bull-fight except to put on that clowning performance, pulling the wool over the eyes of all of them again, including himself. Until he acted the fool, clowning and squirting the pop, she hadn't known it. There was nothing so silly and hopeless in the world as a person bewitched. But until he acted such a fool she hadn't known it had been true of him, and it had been Lois Scanlon herself who caused it. She had held him responsible, never dreaming that something had happened to *him* on the porch—even worse, it would seem, than what had happened to the rest of them. In the play he had said that *he* was God's handyman, and *she* was God's handiwork.

"McKee—" she called, and when he came over she put her hand on his arm, feeling him thick and solid, and wondered again what in the world she might have done if he hadn't been there. To marry, that is. To help her get her feet back on solid ground.

"A cup of coffee and you'll never know what hit you," he said, and of course he was right.

"Bang! Bang!" the boy yelled, and fired his gun. "He's dead."

"Dead?" Scanlon said. "You sure he's dead?" He stared as if he might see, then for the hundredth time said, "If you want to keep him dead you got to pile on the rocks. You got to run the wheels over him. Now why you suppose we did that?"

Scanlon

"Because he was a Mormon," replied the boy, and shot him again.

The old man let it pass. Sometimes he wondered himself if that wasn't at the root of it. That fellow was a Mormon. He'd had too many wives. He probably knew from the first one that he'd come to no good end.

On the sky above him, a clean sheet of glass that looked a little rippled and smoky at the edges, he saw the speck. He nudged the boy and said, "There he is." The boy looked up, saw him, and shot him, but he didn't yell out he was dead. He knew better. At least he'd got around to knowing that. You could shoot your fool head off but you'd never bring down a bird like that.

A bird? It was a bird if a bird could croak like a frog. If a bird could smell like the dead, then it was a bird.

"I tell you—" he began, and of course he had, just that morning—and so many other mornings—he had told the boy about the wind. How it blew the words right out of your mouth. Since there was nothing out there for that wind to blow on, no sails, no windmills,

84

nothing like that, nothing but yourself, you took it personally. Then that river they'd looked forward to, that was there on the map, hadn't a drop of water in it, just a sand so fine it was like powder in an hourglass. They couldn't see the wagons ahead or behind them because of the dust. It hung around the fires like clouds of smoke, since there were always wagons that kept going, and they could hear them coming up with their wheels bone dry, then hear the whips when they went off. Long after they had banked the fires at night the sky would be light, up where they could see it, but down in the canyon the morning and the evening were not so far apart. The wagons were like ants in the neck of a bottle, and all along the trail, wherever you looked, they were busy putting something down, or picking something up. Everybody seemed to have a lot more than they needed, and right beside the trail, where you could reach out and touch them, were sacks of beans and sugar, and slabs of bacon stacked like cords of wood. Back on the plains people would trouble to hide it, thinking they would come back for it later, but there in the canyon they just dumped it beside the trail. Anything that was heavy, that would lighten the wagon, they dumped out first. Some had brought along every fool thing they owned, rocking chairs, tables, and barrels of dishes, and others had big framed pictures they would like for setting up house. Some had brought along books, trunks of fine linen, all the tools they might need for building a home, and you could see what a man valued most in his life from where he put it down. Towards the last you began to see people, friends who had sworn they would never part, or relations who had got too old, or too weak, left to shift for themselves. They weighed too much. So they were just dumped like everything else.

No matter where it was that people had been, or where it was they thought they were going, they

wanted it to be the same as wherever they were from.
They brought along whatever they needed to make
it that way. Cages for birds, furniture and fine clothes,
bolts of calico and dressmaker's dummies, and a man
who had lived near the sea brought with him a diving
bell. When he saw he wouldn't need it and put it
down—another man picked it up. And in that man's
wagon, except for his family, he had none of the
things with which he had started, since he seemed to
like better anything that belonged to somebody else.
Certain other people felt the same way, which was
why they would see, ahead on the trail, what they had
put down themselves a day's ride back. That was why
things traveled faster than people, some of them a lot
farther than the people who had owned them, since
none of the wagons ever stopped to pick people up.

When he was asked about that, Reverend Tennant
said that all of these things were possessed by the
Devil, and all they were doing was delivering them to
him, free of charge. The Devil himself was that fly
speck they saw on the sky. A bird? If a bird could
croak at you like a frog. A bird, if a living thing
could smell like the dead. They could see him wheel,
drawing this circle like a kid would do with a stick on
water, but without any ripples, just this speck at the
center of it. All around them the mountains, not so
much blue as black, the valley like a dead sea in between them, and overhead was this bird—if that was
what it was.

Not a blade of grass, just this brush that was white
as a bone, without leaves on it, the branches like so
many dead and dried roots sticking up in the air. Reverend Tennant went so far as to say that was what it
was. In the Devil's country wouldn't everything naturally be upside down? He pulled up one of the plants
to show them, and sure enough, just as he said, there

was more of the plant beneath the ground than there was above. He said if they could turn it over, the whole valley would look like that. The Lord and the Devil had just switched places, with the Devil upstairs and the Lord in the basement, the Devil naturally being top man in his own house. That was what he said, that was how it looked, but every night he went on praying for rain, although the Devil was the man to pray to in country like that. If the Lord made it rain, it was the Devil who dried it up. He was the one who turned the rivers into sand, and the lakes into salt.

The more the Reverend prayed the drier it got, and one member of the party, a Mr. Criley, spoke up and said that he'd lost all faith in Mr. Wesley's map. He had a map of his own, which he'd bought from an Indian, and this map looked older than the one they had, being torn at the seams, and with a bullet hole in one corner of it. All of the places where there was water were marked with a well. Otherwise they were marked with a skull and crossbones, which led some to believe it must be honest, since a liar wouldn't trouble to point out to them what they didn't want to know. Scanlon knew a liar wouldn't, but it seemed to him the Devil would. It was just the sort of thing a clever sort of Devil would do. That map was just a piece of his handiwork, like the lakes some of them saw, with the shady trees around them, the water cool and shimmering in the high noon light. People wanted to believe in what they saw, so they did. They wanted to believe in Criley's map, so they left the trail, the one made by the wagons, and cut across country on the one that was just on the map.

And that fool bird? What did he do but tag along.

"Why you suppose, boy—" Scanlon barked out, as if he had been talking out loud from the start, "why you suppose that fool bird went along?"

No answer. Hadn't he told the boy that part of it? The Devil went along because he was human—lonely, that is. It put him at a certain disadvantage since he couldn't seem to either take it or leave it, but he had to tag along, like a kid, and see how it worked out.

"I tell you he was human, boy?" he said, but that fool horn, blowing from somewhere, made him crook around and stare up the slope. Like a wall. The canyon had been like that. The cooling sky was pretty much as he remembered it. The wind had not come up—it had just blown away from where they were sitting, sucking the fire out, and rain as hard and dry as pebbles fell from the sky.

"I tell you—" he began, but the boy cried—

"Granpa! Look, granpa!" and stuck the barrel of that gun he had in his ribs. So he did. He got himself turned around and looked. Out on the luminous sand he could see what had fooled him. One of them shimmering lakes.

Boyd

When the boy yelled *look*, Boyd had turned from the bullring—where a new bull had just entered—to watch McKee going down the aisle behind his wife. The trouble with McKee—one of the troubles—was that you couldn't tell the normal run of his talk from his high dry flights of humor. *Don't it take you back, Boyd?* He knew sure as hell it did. But to where? And when? And for chrissakes why? Taken back. Always taken back. Never ahead.

Boyd had not lost his touch—in his bloodless fashion he had just cut two ears, with a fizzing pop bottle—but that too took him back, away back. That too had an antique charm. The derring-do of the non-professional touch. The high wax-winged flights of Icarus Boyd, audacious amateur. The big touch was beyond him. As a touching example, he was still alive. He should have died, fizzing bottle in hand, as he turned to receive the *oles*, as he should have drowned in that sandpit west of Polk. As something in him had. Dr. Leopold Lehmann had pointed that out.

Thanks to the curve of the ring Boyd could watch the McKees, cruising in tandem, head for the exit, good-provider McKee straining a bit at the invisible leash. Refugees from the dust bowl, Sears, Roebuck gothic, wearing the dacron they could wash if they had to, and the expression that might wrinkle a little, but would never wear off. The *little woman*, in this case, an inch or two taller, her lips set as if coated with alum, her elbows tucked in close to keep McKee from latching on. Leaving to the dogs—to worse than the dogs—the apple of her eye, the infant Davy Crock-

ett, along with her father, the mummified effigy of
the real thing. Two carnival attractions, two allegorical figures advertising the latest frontier victories, the
last celluloid effort to turn time back in its flight.
Away back. Where time itself seemed to stop. The
Origin of the Species, Adam & Eve McKee in the Dust-
bowl Garden, full of park benches, with Boyd the
subtle serpent hanging by his knees from the apple
tree. Born to be the upstart, the naughty cupid, the
pocket snatcher, the walker on water, the gray haired
youth who slew the Minotaur with a squirt of pop.

Profession? Hero.

Situation? Unemployed.

In the runway right beneath, the rag still clutched
in his hand, his hair up wild and his pale forehead
sanded, stood the young man with nothing more than
the horn prick on his shirt. The hero. In the orphic
spell of his charmed life. Little or nothing but wonder
on his face. That he was alive? He seemed unaware of
it. His bloodless lip bleeding where he had bitten
down on it himself. The policeman who held him
shook the arm in his grasp as though it was detached,
perhaps a clock that had stopped—the other crooked
a finger to point at the horn prick on his shirt. Smiling. To indicate he would live. To comment on the
irony of it. Beginner's luck? It was clear he was alive
because he was a fool—not in spite of it. If he had
been less a fool he would have come prepared, with
a cloth like a sail, and he would now be dead. Not
having seen the cloth at all the bull had hit him
square, *between* the horns. As they led him away the
crowd rose from their seats, some cheered.

"There's nothing—" said the man across the aisle,
winding the shutter of his camera, "there's nothing the
world loves so much as a goddam fool."

Was that right? Did it explain the current shortage

of love? If so, the world loved the hero as himself,
without his beard and disguises. Without his armor,
but not without his dragon. Just the plain dam fool.
In his heroics a potential bungler, and in his bungling
a potential hero. In him every man loved the hero in
himself. There was no head on which the helmet of
Mambrino would not fit. If the world loved such a
fool, it could be said of Boyd, one of the goddamdest,
that few men in his time had been so well loved.

"That's Ty Cobb's pocket," he would say, when the
Lord asked him what it was he was wearing. In place of
the leaf. In place of the hero, Eagle Scout Boyd.

The origin of this species? A log cabin, preferably.
But that took trees, and there were no trees on the
plains. Only heroes, sheroes, villains, and lumberyards.
Around the lumberyard, like so many shavings, the
clapboard house. On the ground, but not in it, with an
air of having been brought out on a freight car, from
somewhere better, in order to prove that life could be
worse. Protestant. The ornamental ball on the light-
ning rod an act of protest, a finger shaken at the way
the heavens were run. Temporary. A nomad's refuge
where nothing like a tent would anchor, the perma-
nent shelter being the storm cave out in back. A hole
in which to hide, like a ground hog, from the elements.

In spite of that one lived there? No, one lived there
because of it. Only where fools rushed in were such
things as heroes bred. In front of this clapboard house
the long-stemmed grass grew higher than the porch,
where the rain dripped, and at the corner of the
porch a barrel to catch the rain and raise garter snakes.
Three white hairs from a mare's tail, dropped into
the barrel, would give you three snakes. A miracle?
Heavens no. The commonplace way to make snakes.
The natural power of rain in a barrel. The power to
transform went along with this barrel and the clap-

board house. At the front it had a door, a slamming
screen at the back, and at the side a grassy ditch where
the Jewel Tea Wagon would park in the shade while
the Jewel Tea mare would fertilize the grass. Across the
road were the tracks, beyond the tracks the lumberyard where John Crete, Lord of Creation, doled
out houses, miracles, and ice in the summertime. A
red fence went all the way around it, with the CRETE
in white, but the letter R missing where the boards
were removed to put in a metal gate. Down the spur
to the west, wobbly as buggy lanes, the tracks that
led to the bottomless sandpit, circus wagons on flat-
cars, and the buggy seats in the trampled spring grass.
Was that all? The budding hero found it more than
enough. Enough, but not too much. With world
enough and time to get on with it.

On the clapboard house, nailed over the scars from
the quarantine signs for measles and scarlet fever, a
bronze plaque that would read—

Birthplace of
T H E   H E R O
Widely Loved and Known As
A   G O D D A M   F O O L

Down the road from this house, up like a caboose
on concrete blocks, so one could hide *beneath* it, the
home of Walter McKee—

Birthplace of
T H E   W I T N E S S
Without whom there would not have been
A   H E R O

Boyd watched the matador Da Silva, a young man
said to wear false calves, but otherwise fearless, gaze
from the funk hole with beads of sweat on his face.

He followed, with unblinking eyes, the fawn-colored
bull. Too much bull, perhaps? As the first one had
been too little. Backing away, barking at him, one of
the *peones* fanned his face with the cape. Da Silva
watched the sweep of the head, the hooking movement of the horns. A preview of the bull's boxing
style, the way he would fight. Any tendency he had
to lead with the left, hook with the right. The object?
Not to kill the bull—that could be done very neatly
from the funk hole—but to kill him, strictly speaking,
with the cloth. According to the rules. That is to say,
according to the risks. It was not a sport, it was even
less a gamble, the bull would get it no matter how he
gave it, and when he left the ring he would be dead.
To what end then? The textbook manual said *Art.*
The face of Da Silva—not a very good one, isolated
from its body by the boards of the funk hole—the
boyish face of Da Silva made Boyd think of something else. The origin of a species. A thatched roof,
preferably. Inhabited by heroes, sheroes, villains, and
matadors. And the rain barrel? It would give you
more than garter snakes. The ears and tail of a bull,
freshly cut, would give you a hero. A miracle?
Heavens no, an everyday fact. It came perfectly natural to ears and a tail when they were cut like that.
The power to transform went along with the funk
hole, the face, and the cloth.

Birthplace of
THE HERO
Widely Loved and Known As
A GODDAM FOOL

On his way to Mexico Boyd had driven back to see
if the town was still there, if the house was still there,
and if the barrel was still there. They were. Only one
detail was missing. The word CRETE was no longer

stamped on everything. All five letters were now gone
from the lumberyard fence. They were no longer in
gold on the window of the bank, or blown up in
shadow on the library blind. And the House of the
Lord himself? A funeral home. For the convenience
of the heroes who had not panned out, who were still
unemployed.

He had parked his car where the Jewel Tea Wagon
horse had cropped and fertilized the grass. A light
glowed in the second floor window of the clapboard
house. He could see, on the drawn yellow blind, the
shadow of the stovepipe with its goiter-like bulge.
Above this bulge, the damper. It was now turned up.
That, too, had changed, since in his mind it was always
turned down. That stovepipe came up through the
floor from the coke burner in the room below, and
where it bulged like a goiter it would get hot when
the damper was down. He could hear the coke crackle
and settle when he turned it up. But he liked it down.
Not that he wanted it hot. Not that he intended—as
it turned out—to fill the house with smoke. All he
wanted to do by turning the damper was to bring up
the woman who lived below, the way the genie in the
picture would rise out of Aladdin's lamp. She would
come up with her lamp, the wick swimming in oil,
and cross the room like the figures in his dreams, without noises, without so much as taking steps. Holding
the lamp to his face she would see that he was asleep.
He would feel the heat of the chimney on his forehead, catch a whiff of the oil. She would first open
the damper, then turn with the lamp so that the room
darkened behind her, but her snow white hair seemed
to trap the light. During the day it would be piled on
her head, but when she came up with the lamp it
would be in braids. With a silver-handled comb that
rattled when she used it, facing the mirror that no

longer had a handle, she would comb out the tangled ends of her braids. Out would come, like the burrs in a dog's tail, the knotted hairs. When all the hairs stood up, like a brush, she would pass the ends slowly over the chimney, where they would curl at the tips and crackle with a frying sound. Then the smell, as when she singed a chicken over a hole in the kitchen range, or turned the bird, slowly, in the flame of a cob dipped in kerosene.

What did it do?

Something for the hair. That was what she claimed. But it did more than that, certainly, for the boy in the bed. What did he see? More than met the eye. But in this strange transformation, what was transformed? The ceremony of the flame, the crackling and the smell, the hand that passed the taper over the chimney, made this woman something more than an aging Sarah, who had miraculously conceived this Isaac. No wonder the Lord had deprived her of Abraham. A pollen bearer. There had been no further need of him. A load of timber had providentially rolled off a flatcar, crushing him. This timber belonged to John Crete, the Lord's representative, and he saw to it that the child, the young hero, should not want. The word Crete, the Lord's seal of approval, had been stamped on him. Behind the cage at the bank, behind the grain on the scales, behind the corn in the cribs, the beef on the hoof, behind the sun when it set, setting it aright, was the word CRETE. In the beginning was the word. The education of the hero had begun with it.

From where Boyd sat in the car, the motor idling, he could see down the tracks to the grain elevator where the last coat of paint—a fading yellow—was peeling off. Under this coat, shadowy but re-emerging, was the word CRETE. Very much as it emerged, as he sat there staring, on Boyd's mind.

Boyd had begun to wear, before he could walk, the clothes of the Crete boy, who was one year older, and later he was sometimes mistaken for that boy in the street. His name was Ashley. But Boyd seldom set eyes on him. Only his clothes. Ashley Crete was always away somewhere where he grew so fast his clothes were a problem; old clothes were too small, and new things were never worn out. That was left to Boyd. But he never quite grew into, or out of them. A larger size, at that point, would replace the suit he had almost grown into, or the shoes he had not yet broken in. He knew the clothes, but not the boy who had stepped out of them. That boy was in the pictures on the piano or the table in his mother's bedroom, wearing the clothes, shoes, stockings and cap that he would soon send back to Boyd.

Patent leather oxfords, short velvet pants that showed the garter hooks when he was seated, and underwear that proved that Ashley Crete never wet his pants. These clothes were never shortened, since Mrs. Boyd, a believer in true breeding, was sure that Boyd would grow faster if he knew that he was short of the mark. If the shoes had not been larger, the sleeves longer, Boyd might have stopped growing in his fifth or sixth year, but he *had* to grow, knowing the larger size was waiting for him. One might even say that he went on growing—until it was not. That would be wrong, an oversimplification, but when Ashley Crete stopped walking on the water—of Boyd's imagination—Boyd stopped walking on it himself. But not his mother. No, she had kept the faith. So long as she was alive Boyd had been supported on a raft of newspaper clippings, which kept him in touch with the Gods in her pantheon.

The only God that had failed had been Boyd himself.

Although he had started well. Like a house afire, in some respects.

The day he went over the fence and got himself a pocket he had been armed with nothing but his intentions, and wearing the first pair of pants worn only by himself. A test case. To see if he could run this show by himself. On a Sabbath day like this one, in seats along the rail such as these were, with a bullring featuring Tyrus Raymond Cobb, the Georgia Peach.

What had been his object? To get a foul ball autographed. One that had been hit by the master hitter, one that Boyd had caught. To get it signed. That was the gist of it. But in the riot that followed, the ball field swarming with hundreds of small fry, each with a mission, Boyd had forgotten the foul ball he set off with, hooked on the hero's pants. He had taken a goring, but he had cut one ear, nevertheless. It was there in the form of a pocket to the great man's pants.

What he had had in mind—or below his mind, so that it occurred without complications—was not to get the ball signed, which might have been done in the hotel lobby, or the shade of the dugout, but to get it signed according to the rules. To get it transformed. And this had occurred. A stranger transformation than he had thought. Not merely a foul ball into a pocket, but a pocket into a winding sheet where the hero lay, cocoon-like, for the next twenty years. Out of this world, in the deep-freeze of his adolescent dreams. The object was transformation, but it had stopped where it should have begun. There was not one bull, but many, each transformation called for another, or the hero remained like the music in Baron Munchausen's horn. Like Boyd, that is. Snug in his flannel winding sheet.

He watched the matador, the young magician Da Silva, step from the wings of his imagination, erect but abstract in his pearl gray suit of light. On the column of his spine, like a mourning capitol, the funereal hat. He did not look up to see, nor seem to care about, the bull. The beast stood, a little winded and perplexed, with his rear end to the fence, the non-existent corner. Like so many brushes in the palette on his hump, were the ribboned darts. Two of them sticking up. But Da Silva? He stood alone with himself. He came to face them, doffing his hat, bending back from his hips like a floating diver, and with a fine carelessness tossed the hat over his shoulder, like a pinch of salt.

Did the bull feel that? He pawed the sand where he stood. Da Silva let him wait, working like a painter with the folds of the cloth, the way it draped, then he drew on the sand, with his eyes, the line that the bull would take. He took it, fanning out the cloth, then wheeling as if his master had whistled.

Ole!

The noise that Boyd had made himself left him deaf. He had its flavor in his mouth.

The bull charged from the left, then the right, then again from the left, with each charge shorter, each turn sharper, until he stood twisted on his own spine. Screwed around until he faced the direction he had come from, brought to a standstill, unable to go two directions at once.

And the matador? At this point he had turned away. As from a still life, an arrangement that would remain as he had left it, the scene transformed into a frieze of permanence. The matador a magician, holding the wand to which was attached the magic cloth, behind which the double transformation had taken place. Word into flesh, and the flesh itself into myth. He came toward them, his body buoyant, the head straining at the leash that held it, the face tipped to catch the shower of praise that came down like light. The praise making a roar, a siphoning sound that swirled about him, creating a vortex, a still point where he stood alone with himself. Not unlike Paula Kahler in that he saw, in the swirl of faces, his own reflection, and in the roar heard only what he wanted to hear. He stood before them in a trance, his hand upraised to catch the charge of their admiration, to mark the spot where the next transformation would take place.

The bull, coming up behind him, put it into effect.

Lehmann

In Guanajuato, on the way down, Lehmann had taken sick. During the long night it had occurred to him, with the clarity of a hallucination, that he was not sick with a bug, or from food, or anything that he could *catch*. He was sick from Mother Mexico herself. From her exhausting extremes, her legerdemain, in which the limbs perform tricks without the body, from her excessive beauty as well as from her poverty and decay. It was simply too much for a pasteurized stranger from the north. Not merely what he had seen, but what he had seen and repressed. *Why order your thoughts?* Mussolini had asked, and Lehmann had always found it a disturbing question. Why indeed? But he had learned why that night, thanks to Mexico. If he could not order his thoughts, he was sick. It had been his failure to order his thoughts that made him ill. The nausea had come as a form of analysis. Intestinal Freud. Followed by relief, if not a cure. What his mind could not stomach, for very long, had to come up.

Mrs. McKee had reminded him of that—Mrs. McKee, with her head lolling on his shoulder, having fainted, Lehmann was sure, of the same sort of thing. Not bulls, not pyramids and altitude, but Mexico.

Which was certainly why—Lehmann reflected, hearing the click of her knitting needles—Paula Kahler was always in the best of health. Everywhere. Since all places were the same. The same reflection gazed at her from all of the mirrors. She had been sick to the death—she had died, that is—and passed over to the other side. From there all things looked the same. They were small as a rule, thought to be helpless, and of one sex. There were no males in Paula Kahler's brave new world.

Baby lambs, kittens, collie pups, cows in the manger, birds in the trees, but no bulls, no roosters, and no rams. Better yet, *little* things. *Anything* that was small enough. Ants, for instance. My God, what a time he had with ants. Couldn't get her past them if she saw them crossing a walk. They were not like bulls. There was no easy way to tell about the boy ants.

This roar that swelled up around her, the build up of the *ole's*, like a cheering section, she did not hear any more than her cats heard the noise in the street. But the faintest scratch, the soundless fall of seed from the cage of her canary, any sound that *meant* something, like water dripping, she never missed. Did she hear him *thinking?* Her gaze seemed to focus on something insubstantial over the ring. He looked himself, saw the young man with his hand upraised, as if in blessing, and it led him to wonder, he almost turned to *look* for the bull. He didn't have to, since right at that moment man and bull were one. The youth seemed to grow out of the bull's neck and shoulders, as Lehmann had so often dreamed it, a living centaur, the archetypal man growing out of the beast. For a moment he seemed to soar, his arms spread wide, the cloth unfurling in the wind beside him, his eyes wide with the wine of astonishment. Would he fly? Would he go winging off like the flying horse?

Lehmann himself had stood up—a man of little faith, he had thrown up his own arms—to catch him when he toppled like Nike from her pedestal. The bull, as if stunned and witless, stood to one side. He did not follow up his advantage. Did he consider it one? Having been, at that moment, more than a bull, he was at a loss what to do next. Man *and* Bull had both been shot down—Lehmann would tell you—at the moment of flight. Resolving and not resolving the anguished dilemma of human life. Man, his arms spread wide, could only take wing on the thrust of his past, and at the risk of toppling forward on his face. Bull into Man was followed, too often, by Man into Ghost. The horn of the dilemma—like the one at his side—was that it led to flight.

He placed his hand on her arm, since Paula Kahler, the true bird that never was, having taken flight once might see fit to take it again. He watched them lift the young man—the stain spreading on the inside of the thigh, where one hand gripped him—but the shock on the faces of the men supporting him. On his own face sweat, a patch of sand as if he had been down at the beach, napping, and they were carting him down to the water to rinse him off.

A row or two behind him a man's voice said, "Well, you asked for it, baby. How does it feel?"

How did it? Dr. Leopold Lehmann, the male Blavatsky as Boyd affectionately called him, sometimes thought he knew, although he had never been gored himself. He had the touch. He had been there, so to speak. If Paula Kahler had been able to vouch for anything, she would have vouched for that.

According to his income tax, a dependent, classified as his housekeeper, Paula Kahler was the woman —strange to say—in Dr. Lehmann's life. A case—he had once noted down—of arrested development. A simpleminded wonder and affection for childish things. A nature that refused to acknowledge the aggressive elements. Maleness, that is. Maleness being at the heart of it.

Her possessions—an old wicker bag to which she had strapped a ribless umbrella—contained nothing of interest but her large collection of miniature animals.

Hundreds of them, a regular zoo, with one unusual feature. They were all females. The males, and their aggressive ways, had been weeded out. Beginning with herself.

At one point a toy Ark, sold to children at Christmas, had been added to the wildlife haven in her room. Didn't that make it clear? Could it have been a mere accident? Having rounded up the female of the species she was prepared, like Noah, to sail off after the flood and start a new world. Lehmann had been apprehensive for months. He locked her in when he left the apartment, trailed her around when she shopped. Then the answer had crossed his mind one summer night. He, Leopold Lehmann, was the brave new world himself. She had already sailed off, and arrived in it. The female-haunted rooms of his apartment, forever burbling with the voice of the female turtle, the male shored up in her dreams and in other responsibilities. At that point the case of Paula Kahler—as a case—officially closed.

A month later it reopened. Unofficially.

In the wicker bag he had stored in the closet—he had to take it down when mice were found in it—he had come upon a postcard, slipped into the lining, addressed to Paul Kahler, Camp Hastings, Illinois. It was signed by Warren Shults, of Chicago, Illinois. He had written the card from the Larrabee Y.M.C.A.

Lehmann had walked down the street to the St. George Hotel, where they kept a rack of phone books in the lobby, and looked in the Chicago directory for the name of Shults. He found it. He was still at the Larrabee Y.M.C.A. On the pad in the booth Lehmann noted down the number—not quite clear in his mind what he meant to do with it—then turned back to the phone book and glanced at the K's. There were many Kahlers, but only one Paul Kahler, and, strange to relate, the address was the same. Paul Kahler and Warren Shults were listed at the same number. The same Y.M.C.A.

Lehmann had walked to the bar, where he had himself a stiff one, then he had come back to the booth, put through the call.

The voice replying said, "Good evening, Larrabee Y.M.C.A."

"I woot lak to spik to Paul Kahler," Lehmann had said. At tense moments his speech—it was no language—got considerably worse.

"Kahler?" came the reply. "We have no Kahler listed."

"Ware coot I get in tudge?" Lehmann had inquired.

"Anybody know of a Kahler—a Paul Kahler?" He had turned and asked the question of someone. Lehmann heard the answer.

"Paul *who?*"

"Kahler," the voice repeated.

"Connect the line to my office," came the reply, and Lehmann heard the plug switch him over. He waited a moment, then the voice cried, "Paul? Is that you Paul?"

"I am werry zorry," Lehmann replied. "I am nod Paul. I was callink to fine him."

There was no reply. Lehmann thought the connection had been broken and said, "Operador. Oh, operador!"

"Shults, speaking," said the voice. "Paul Kahler is missing."

Lehmann thought a moment, then took the plunge. "Thod is wot I understand, Mr. Shoolts," he said. "Maybe he iss no lonker so missink?"

"Hermann!" said Mr. Shults. "Is that you, Hermann?"

"My name iss Lehmann," he replied, "and I may haf some noose aboud Paul Kahler."

"You knew him? You have seen him?"

"Thod iss the gueschun," said Lehmann.

"Slight and frail," said Mr. Shults, "blond hair, blue eyes. Last seen with his brother Hermann."

"Woot there be any phodographs?" Lehmann asked.

"Here on my desk—" said Mr. Shults, then stopped. Lehmann waited while he thought it over.

"If I coot zee zom pig-chur," Lehmann put in.

"I'm afraid I can't let you have it," said Shults. "Group picture. Several of them in it. But you're welcome to come and look at it." Lehmann did not speak up, and Shults said, "He is alive then. You have seen him?"

"If it iss the zame person, he iss fery mudge alife," Lehmann said.

"If you could come—" Shults interrupted, then said, "Where are you? If you could come by this evening?"

"Led us mag it tomorrow efenink," he replied, and while the voice of Shults was still talking, telling him about the street cars, and the El, Lehmann had hung up. He had to hurry in order to catch the night train.

He hadn't slept. He had sat up in the coach, since there were no berths available, staring out the window at the places his clients came from. Small towns, most of them, where the lights burned over empty corners, the houses dark with the dreams they would ask Lehmann to analyze. As Boyd had cracked, they were all great places to be *from*. But that, of course, was the dilemma. They left, but they never got away. Trailing along behind them, like clouds of glory, were the umbilical cords. On his mind's eye Lehmann saw them like the road lines on a map. Thousands stretched to reach Chicago. Millions stretched to reach New York.

The train had let him off in the heart of the labyrinth. He had taken a cab to the near north side, a neon jungle with a gold coast trimming, and rented a hotel room within a block of the Y.M.C.A. The bell-hop, an elderly man, with the yolk of an egg drying in his mustache, led him down a creaking uncarpeted hall to the room at the front. As they entered the room a warning bell on a drawbridge began to clang. Lehmann watched the shadow of the bridge, like a hand, move on the yellow blinds. Because the air in the room seemed stale he lowered the transom, then tried to raise a window, a cloud of sparkling dust puffing out from the curtain when he brushed it with his hand. He had leaned there a moment, gazing at the street, the barge he could see drifting on the river, and the honking lines of traffic blocked by the bridge. He could feel the building tremble, as if with rage, when a street car passed.

Had something stopped? Were they waiting for the heart of the city to start? Above the warning bell, the idling motors, Lehmann thought he could hear the lapping of the river, just as he could smell, above the stench of the city, the sewage in the canal. As the shadow of the bridge moved on the blind the honking increased, reached a point of frenzy, and then like a pack of unleashed hounds, the traffic began to flow.

He lay out on the bed just to rest for a bit, not to sleep. Did he doze off? Perhaps; something woke him up. He was aware of the vibration in the bed that never left the room. The springs on which he lay gave off a sound like wind in a harp. Over his head, like a clouded eye, a frosted bulb suspended from the ceiling, with a knot looped in the cord to shorten it. He was able to see that the cord was lumpy with flies. That the bulb sustained an even, somewhat elliptical, swing. This movement did not trouble the flies, however, any more than the movement of the earth, tipped on its axis, seemed to trouble the man on the bed. He felt, at the moment, suspended in space himself. That might have been the heat, which was bad, the droning of the traffic in his ears, or the calendar on the wall at the foot of the bed. The date? It was May, 1931. A red-cheeked child tirelessly licked by a long-haired dog. On the sky an airplane, symbol of his future, in the background a mother, symbol of his past, but in the eternal present he would go on being licked by his faithful dog.

It struck Lehmann—it struck the person, that is, that he seemed to be at that particular moment—as if he had rented this room in a time capsule. Time—of the other variety—seemed to have stopped. Lehmann had been stored away, forever, with this small piece of it. A cord lumpy with flies, a bed that sang like a harp, a basin in the corner that smelled of urine, and a calendar dated May, 1931. These things, that is to say, were the eternal ones. They would not change. They would grow neither down nor up. They were immortal, and they represented the everlasting things in nature, as well as the everlasting nature of things. The eternal moment in the shifting tides of life. The eternal personality of sweet and sour, pleasure and pain. The changeless dreams of love and affection, licked forever the changeless face of the young, in which the changing past and future were always the same. In the dream, that is, began the irresponsibility. The sleeper awake, the shadow on the blind, the fly-clotted cord, and the drip in the basin that signified life, death and erosion in the mind. What one would find, that is, at the heart of the labyrinth. A hotel room, a guest for the night, the gift Bible with the red-stained leaves, and the figure in the carpet long ago worn into the cracks in the floor. The bed itself lipped with a spout, as if to pour out the sleeper, and the door with hooks on which to hang the empty days, the sleepless nights. And at the heart of this capsule was Leopold Lehmann, timeless man.

The way a fruit would drop, with no wind blowing,

one of the flies on the lumpy cord lost his grip, fell, and bounced on Lehmann's chest. Through one cocked eye he saw the creature on its back, the legs in the air. Dead? Lehmann put out his hand, a finger cocked to snap it—then paused, and returned the hand to his side. Something he remembered. Something he had seen Paula Kahler do. A fly presumed dead, given up for lost, found by her floating in the flower water, had been revived by her with the sun and a sprinkling of salt. Lehmann had observed it with his own eyes. The fly sprinkled with salt, then placed in the sun, and after a moment one leg had wiggled, then another, pushing the salt to one side. With a toothpick, she had helped him to his feet. He had groomed a bit, before leaving, stroking his wings with his feather dusters, then buzzing his motor in an experimental flight. Paula Kahler had then opened the screen and the fly flew out.

Lehmann had thought it a fine example of the saintly and simple-minded, saving the fly so that *he* would have to swat it again. Man had to choose. He couldn't go on kidding himself. If it was man or fly—Lehmann had once more raised his hand, cocked the finger—when he saw it move. To check on that he held his breath. Squinting, he saw a twitch. No more, but a twitch. He took a quick breath and waited. Another twitch. Two legs, now working together. Had the dead come to life? Or was it a question of altitude? The heat, or the poisonous air that prevailed up near the ceiling, had been too much—so he had fallen to his proper sphere. He twitched again, as if sprinkled with salt. Easily, as well as painlessly, Lehmann could have finished him off. Enlightened self interest? That was the term for it. And if it was a matter of choice, that was the time. But he held off, he reduced his breathing lest the fly rock off the platform, and drop into less favorable circumstances.

Why? With the fly in *that* condition he had no choice. Lehmann, that is. He had killed, in his time, thousands of flies, and he would swat any fly with the strength to attack him, but he could not swat this fly on its back. As helpless, there on his shirt front, as man himself. Groggy with the heat, poisoned with the air, a nervous wreck from the noise and the vibration, what he needed, speaking fly to man, was help. As a man, Lehmann felt obliged to give it to him. The fly's proper business was to lump light cords, ping on screens, contaminate food, and whenever the opportunity offered make men miserable. And the man's proper business?

Lehmann had closed his eyes. In a book he had read having to do with some brothers, all of them typical half-mad Russians, one of them had had a dream that Lehmann could never forget. This one had dozed off for just a moment—the way Lehmann had just dozed off himself—and he had this dream that hardly seemed connected with anything else. He was off somewhere, on the steppes, as Lehmann had a feeling of great bleakness, when this sleigh he was in went by these people standing near the road. Just about the saddest collection of people anyone had ever seen. All of them thin and dirty, their faces off-color, and one of the women of the party had this child which she held to her dried-up breasts. The man in the sleigh asked the driver what the devil was wrong with them. Then this driver answered, "*It's the babe weeping,*" and the man in the sleigh, along with Lehmann, was struck by the driver using the word *babe*. There was more pity in it. As there was between Lehmann and this fly on his chest. In the room he felt the presence of a strange personality. One that was part of the room, the enduring personality of life itself. It joined him, sad as it seemed, in the pity life seemed to feel in the presence of such a fugitive thing as life. Not just pity for Lehmann, nor for flies, but for pity itself.

He lay there till he heard, pinging the blind, the fly that was no longer on his chest, and to avoid a show-down he got up and left the room. He walked the few blocks to the Y.M.C.A., where the lights had been broken out of the sign, and he had to choose between a Men's and a Boys' entrance. He chose the Boys', opened the door, and stepped into the draft of chlor-inated water blowing down the hall from the swim-ming pool. A tall thin man stood in the lobby, twirling a chain of keys. He held a small numbered ball in one hand, and spoke to a tough looking boy.

"The ball is not *my* ball, Vito," he was saying, "the floor is not *my* floor, or you could bounce and roll the ball all that you liked." He paused there, then added, "If it *was* my ball, you could have it, if it *was* my floor, you could bounce it, but it isn't *my* ball, it's *your* ball to have and to keep."

Seeing Lehmann in the door he said, "Next door is the Men's Section."

"I'm Dr. Lehmann—" Lehmann had said. "I called you in regart—" but that had been enough. Mr. Shults had stopped swinging the keys, stepped over and gripped his hand.

"If you'll step back to my office, Dr. Lehmann," he said, and led him by the elbow, as he would have the boy, down the hall to where the smell of the chlor-inated water was very strong. With one of the keys on the long chain he opened the door.

That horn—hearing the blast on the horn Lehmann glanced up as if to see a bull enter—but the entrance gates were closed. The bull he saw was dead. The mules were dragging the fawn-colored body on a tour of the ring. There was applause, and Lehmann joined it, slapping his bright red mittens together, in spite of the fact that Boyd had snickered at such a thing. The bull was dead. What good did it do the bull?

"It iss nod for the bool, which it det," Lehmann had said, "but for Lehmann, who muss go on lifink."

There was more pity in it. There was now that he had thought of it.

The trouble with the bullfight, McKee was thinking, was that where other things ended, it didn't. You saw one accident, then you had to sit back and see another one. But the truth was, he liked it. More the way they came in, than the way they went out. If they had a suggestion box at the gate he'd suggest that they throw a tarp over the dead one. He always had the feeling, dead or not, that they didn't like the flies.

McKee

Take that hog he'd shot—it made his own eyes itchy just to see the flies. Like a swarm of bees around the pail full of his blood. Settled on it like they'd drowned. Like a bucket of dead flies more than anything else.

"Hot cup of coffee," he said, giving her elbow a pinch, "and you'll never know what hit you."

A lot of truth in that. They'd given him coffee when he shot that hog. It was the coffee that made his stomach quiet. If it hadn't been for that he would have whooped his breakfast up. Ham in it from the last hog his uncle had shot. It wasn't till he'd shot the hog that eating ham began to give him the hives.

Hearing the shouts—it sounded to McKee like the word for "oleomargerine," the short one—he turned to see what it was he had missed. The bull had run at the fellow but missed him. There he still was. The bull had two of these darts in his hump like someone had shot arrows at him. *That* he had missed. When he came back he would watch for that. The arrows had got him pretty bloody and some of it had rubbed off on the bullfighter's tights. When McKee shot the hog

112

there had not been a drop till they cut him all up, which was later, but he didn't bleed a drop of blood through that hole in his head. It had stayed just as round and black as his eyes had been. Not a drop of it till his uncle, with the dishpans to catch the blood in, sliced his throat so his heart would help pump his own blood out.

This was where? Boyd had asked him. As well he might. McKee doubted it himself. Texas. The panhandle part of it. McKee had gone down in a day coach with some devil's food cake wrapped in wax bread paper for this Uncle Dwight of his he had never seen. He'd waked up in Amarillo where the sky was supported on these giant posts. Oil derricks. Highest things he'd ever seen. With the land floating on the oil beneath them, which helped McKee to explain it. The way the country seemed to roll like the floors in amusement parks. McKee had gone down there a boy, fifteen, and come back a man.

The train he came in on blocked off the crossing, so that his uncle, who had come in to meet him, wasn't there to meet him until the train pulled out. He didn't climb from the buggy, or say *Hello, Walter,* but just put down his brown hand, as though they'd already met, and McKee had come home after a day or two somewhere else. But he did say one thing. "Kid—" he said, "you ever shoot a hog?" Then he grinned, showing the caps of his teeth, and McKee could see the dirt packed around the roots and the dust like talcum powder in the creases near his eyes. The man who invented the dust bowl had been up that morning, working on it.

Nor had his uncle's place been a farm in any sense McKee understood it; just a two room shack, with a low row of sheds, but no trees or barns. No cows, pigs, horses, or anything like that. There were a few chickens, but they were seldom in the yard since the wind down there would blow them away. The only sign that anybody lived there was the lamp in the window at night, and the clothes flapping on the line during the day. The noise the tractor made seemed to blow over from somewhere else.

It had rained down there one winter. Nobody knew why. But his uncle, the winter it rained, had made forty thousand dollars off the land he had rented, which he had plowed up and planted with winter wheat. The next winter he had added a room to the shack. The hired man had lived and slept in it; but it didn't rain that winter, nor the next, and when the hired man left, McKee had taken his place. If it rained he would make enough money to be a farmer himself.

His window looked out on a yard as clean and hard as the floor boards in the kitchen, with the outhouse standing at the edge of the first plowed strip. Fencing in the outhouse was the row of milk cans used to fuel the tractor, which was always left running since the nights were cold and it was hard to start. It struck McKee as alive, the way it would cough, snort and backfire like it was dying of something, and the way it would shake like a dog that was tired and wet. Like the wind, the coughing never stopped. A perpetual thing, like day and night, and if it dropped down, or the wind lulled it, McKee would wake out of a sound sleep knowing something was wrong. He would lie there awake, hardly breathing, till he heard it coughing again.

There was always this wind but hardly any whine since there was nothing for it to blow on, no trees overhead, or dead leaves to sweep the ground. It was when the wind stopped that he heard it, like a quick intake of breath, and the house would ease back like a sleeper turning in bed. There was nothing to blow on, but he had seen the cats, on the moonlight nights when they went about their business, cross the yard on their bellies as if stalking invisible game. The wind he couldn't see would blow them like kites if they stood up. Full grown hens would sail like bonnets till they caught, like tumbleweed, on the stretch of chicken wire that was put up just to keep them from blowing away. The nights there was a moon it seemed to rise right there in the yard, between the house and the privy, and light up the winter plain with the glow from its backside. The land seemed to fall away like the sea from a swell, rippling where the grass still grew on it, or the white-faced cattle stood in rows along the wire fence. Over this moon one night, right out of the blue, drifted a strange cloud. Where did it come from? McKee had made it himself. It was born in the plume of dust that rose from the plows.

On the tractor at night he could see the lights, thirty miles away, where oil had been found, and in the dawn light the rabbits, as if blinded by it, would get caught in the discs. Smart ones would hop from the furrows, just ahead of the noise, and then crouch to watch him pass, big-eyed as mounted trophies, their ears smoothed flat. The far lights looked as near as the rabbits, but when he threw a clod at something it seemed to rise, hang still for a moment, then drop at his feet. What was wrong? Space. He had no way of measuring it. Things were not at all, out there, as they seemed. The mud caked to his gums became part of his teeth, and a film of dust, soft as face powder, sifted through his clothes and made his body soft to touch. He learned, the hard way, not to wash it off. Water left him chapped and sore, the dust left him soft. He learned to sleep in his socks, his flannel underwear, the shirt that was pinned and hard to unbutton, and to dress in the dark that he knew to be morning. How did he know that? The sun rose, like he did, when the tractor coughed in the yard. Dawn came when the lamp glowed at the cracks in the kitchen door.

Those clouds he saw, drifting like smoke, would one day cover Nebraska, like a smog, and make the sun as red as a bolt hole over New York. Not that McKee knew that. He never knew anything. Not unless Boyd told him, or he read it in something like the *Reader's Digest*. He had to come to a bullfight to remember he had shot a hog. Anything having to do with Boyd he seemed to remember as if it had just happened, but he forgot it if it just had to do with McKee.

"Here's where they keep 'em penned, Lois," he said, and leaned over the fence to look at the bulls. He counted five. That meant they kept on hand some extra ones. In case one turned up like the one Boyd had squirted with the pop. McKee would say the beef steers on his son's ranch ran half again as big as the bulls he was seeing—but they had no fight in them. How did you explain that? What was it about a bull that made him want to fight? Some of the bulls he had seen were so fat they couldn't mount a cow, if they had to, and some of them didn't even seem to want to, which was worse. If it wasn't for artificial insemination, bulls like that would go out of business. The only fun they got out of it was eating, but it seemed to be enough.

"Little dark one here—" he said, when she didn't come over, "is not much bigger than that hog I mentioned."

He had never told her about that hog. She had never asked. He gave her a chance to ask about him now—she knew very well that a bull was bigger—but she wasn't up to snuff or she would have pinned him down about that. One sure way to tell if she was off her feed was when she let things pass.

You ever shoot a hog, kid? his uncle had said, and the day it drizzled they went over to do it. The hog belonged to his uncle but had been rented out to a family named Gudger, who had the corn to feed him. Also quite a bit of garbage, since there were eleven of them. The drizzly day had made it seem as though they went over under water, since nothing changed, the wheels turned, and the matted grass flowed under the buggy like a muddy stream. When he looked up and around they always seemed to be standing still. Sometimes the white-faced cattle were there at the fence as if they had been painted on it, other times they weren't, but it was always the same cattle, and the same fence. They saw the Gudger tree, sticking up like a sail, long before they got to it. The bleak gabled house, with the boarded windows, was like a caboose left somewhere on a siding, and behind this house the sky went up like a wall. The world seemed to end. The house itself looked vacant, but when they got in the yard a swarm of small kids, hooting like Indians, ran out like they'd been waiting to ambush them. They had old knives without handles, and the kids without knives had jagged pieces of glass. McKee was bigger and stronger, with the gun there in his lap, but it gave him a turn.

They had the hog out in back of the house, in a pen, and beneath this old tree in the yard, which was dead at the top, they had a pit of steaming water in an old bathtub. The kids needed the bath, but the water was there for the hog. Once McKee had got around to shooting him, that was where he would be dipped. With their glass blades and knives the kids would scrape all the hair off him. McKee had seen big pigs, and he had seen fat hogs, but this one, propped up like a barrel, struck him as bigger and fatter than any hog he had ever seen. They hadn't fed him any corn that day since it would only be lost in his stomach, not having had the time to turn itself into pork or fat. When his Uncle Dwight had held up a yellow ear, a big one with the tassel waving, the hog had grunted and waddled a step or two toward the fence.

"You let him move in close," his uncle said, "then shoot him between the eyes."

That was all right with McKee—he stood fingering the trigger and waiting for the hog to move in close, when this uncle of his, without aye, yes or no, took this ear of yellow corn and stuck it right in his pants. In his fly, that is, since he had a button off right at that point. The big yellow ear of corn stuck out in the air like something else. All the little Gudgers hooted and roared, the little girls as well as the boys, and McKee had stood there with the tassel of the thing tickling him.

"Here you are, kid," his uncle said, then lowered one of the poles in the fence for him, so he could climb in without dropping the ear of corn. "Stand there till he spots it, kid," he said, "and when he moves in close, you shoot him. You hear me, boy?"

Had McKee nodded his head? He didn't remember. All he remembered was hearing it. He just stood there in the pen until the hog, sniffing the air, waddled over toward him, moving in so close McKee could almost touch him with the barrel of the gun. Who had fired it? McKee himself had no memory of it. He saw the hole, the eye that was like the center of the target, but he had no memory of putting it there himself. The hog did not move, he stood like McKee, his legs spread as if waiting for something, and one of the flies on his snout crawled back and sniffed at the hole. Did he crawl in? McKee was inclined to think that he did.

They strung him up to this tree, dipped him in the bathtub, shaved him down till he was pink and white all over, then cut off his head and propped it in a bucket with the snout sticking up. Over a fire they built in the yard they cooked down the soft parts, the pork shoulders, and stored the pieces in the fat that drained off into heavy lard pails. The light from the fire lit up the yard, the house with the windows boarded, and the swarm of hungry little Gudgers, every one of them shiny with fat. McKee had eaten no pork, his face was clean, but the smell of the fat was thick in his head, like the drone the flies made when they rose up, like hornets, from the pail of blood. He felt that he too was being cooked down, like parts of the hog. He was taking the cure when the wind blew the wood smoke over him. At his back, when he turned to look, the rimless plain lay under the moon, and the grass was the leaden color of a dead sea. The house was an ark, adrift upon it, and here and there, in the hollow of a wave, lights would sparkle as if a handful of stars had dropped. In front of him was the fire, the swarm of Gudgers, and strung up as if lynched was the body of the hog. But not all of him. There was some in the fat, and his head was in the pail. The snout up, the lip curled as if grinning, the third eye he had still open, which led McKee to feel that something in the hog hadn't really died. His head. His head was an onlooker, like McKee. Both McKee and the hog seemed to share the same feelings. That it was a joke. But it was not on the hog. Who then? It was on McKee. McKee with his gun and that fool ear of corn sticking out of his fly. He hadn't killed the hog, the hog had laughed himself to death. The sight of a youngster like McKee with that big ear of corn in his fly had called for one more eye than he had, and that he had got. Thanks to McKee. The better, that is, to die laughing at him.

In the cool of the night the Gudgers had all curled up like dogs, and slept together, but McKee and the hog had kept the vigil—the joke, that is. The lip of the hog, McKee could tell you, curled up till all of his teeth were showing, and there were times when McKee heard him laugh with a snort. Toward morning some honking geese flew over, some of them so low he could see the fire on them, but until a rooster crowed he wasn't sure at all but what he'd dreamed it all up. Was it any wonder he'd kept that story to himself? McKee with the corn in his fly, that hog with his curled lip grinning, and the night itself, as Mrs. McKee would have put it, more or less bewitched. Quite a bit like that summer night on the Scanlon porch. As much or more was going on, McKee could tell you, as the night Gordon Boyd, McKee's best friend, kissed the lips of the girl McKee himself had never kissed. And the girl? McKee could tell you something else. She'd married McKee, but she hadn't really kissed another man in her life.

"McKee," she said.

When it was flat, like that, he knew he must have been rude. He doffed his hat, tipped his face back, smiling. He didn't recognize the man in the transparent raincoat till he heard his voice.

"Today is the tomorrow you worried about yesterday," said Mr. Cole. That referred to the fact that McKee had spoken to him yesterday. About the bullfight. He hadn't been too sure about Mrs. McKee. They single filed through the gate to where Mrs. Cole was holding up a porch lamp she thought of buying.

"*Zinko—?*" said Mrs. Cole. "Harry, does he mean his money or ours?"

"You buy everything here," said Mr. Cole, "what you going to do in Acapulco?"

They left them to decide and walked down the street to where he'd parked the car. McKee was able to see they still had hubcaps on one side of it. Man from Abilene was saying that he had all four wheels taken off his car.

"Well, here we are, Lois," he said, opened the door, then just stood there, a smile on his face, waiting for what he knew she would say.

Mrs. McKee

"If anything should happen to that *boy*—" she said, and saw his mouth pucker, like a hen's bottom. Into it, like a cork, he put the wet end of his cigar. Before she heard what she knew he was about to say, she pressed the automatic button that rolled up the window. A goldfish, his lips still puckered, he stood there a moment staring at her, then he made a face to indicate he would be right back.

From the rear—the rear of McKee, from the beginning, had been a problem—the way his hands hung down as if his legs, or something, were too short. No hat he ever wore, including this straw one, covered the back of his head as well as the front, but she had never noticed *that* spot before, the way she did down here. Hair—everybody seemed to have it, nobody ever lived long enough to lose it, and when he had his hat off McKee looked like a person who had just got well. Only nurses, or people who were still sick, ever looked at him. What had Alice Morple said? *Honey, anyhow you haven't had that worry*. And she certainly hadn't. Not once. Not a suspicion in more than thirty years.

But had it ever crossed the ninny's mind to have a suspicion himself? Boyd? No, he called *that* something else. He left her alone in such places as Sanborn's. He let her sit in the parks. And here in the very shadow of the bullring, he let her wait in the car. Alone—if she brought it up he would say it had a heater and radio in it—when she had had *young* men, in the San-born's lobby, take her arm like a tomato they were feeling to see if it was ripe. McKee smiling. The way he did that night on the porch.

When Mr. Arnold Clokey, the science teacher from Red Wing, Minnesota, took a liking to her, McKee had actually egged the poor man on. A giant of a man—with whatever it is that made such big men have smooth, baby faces—Mr. Clokey liked the same sort of things in Mexico she liked herself. Pottery, baskets, and those strawberries with the thick sweet cream. McKee seemed to think that any man his own age would feel the same way he did, or at least feel that way about his own wife.

"You two go ahead and fool around—" he said, when they met at that place in Cuernavaca, and just sat there in the square while they went off to fool around. Mr. Clokey had colored to the roots of his hair, which he at least had, and which made him quite attractive, and they had actually fooled around in some of those side streets until nearly dark. Mr. Clokey knew a little more Spanish than she did, having been down once before, in the '30's, and in the course of their walk she got to know him fairly well. He confided in her—as he put it himself—what it was that had brought him down there, although it was a foolish thing for him to indulge in at the time. He had *flown* down, his object being to make a photographic record of the types of people, in Kodacolor, that he could use in his science class. That was why he seemed to be so cluttered up with cameras, tripods and such things. The camera club of Red Wing had loaned him the equipment, and he had gone into debt to acquire some lenses, since he wanted to make sure his trip was a success. To save money he was living with Earl Hornick, a member of the art department, who wanted to do nothing but paint water colors for three weeks. Mr. Clokey had known Earl Hornick for years, had seen him every day in the school cafeteria, without somehow noticing a very small thing. Earl Hornick whistled under his breath all the time. More or less a hiss, like a tire leaking, without much tune or rhythm to it, and he began in the morning and went on hissing like that all day. It had brought Mr. Clokey to the point where he had to do something. In a joshing manner, so as not to hurt his feelings, Mr. Clokey had said, "Earl, you like to sell that whistle?" merely to draw his attention to the fact that it was always going on. Mr. Hornick, however, had taken offense. "There must be something eating you—" he said to Mr. Clokey, "if you let a little friendly whistling upset you."

Mr. Clokey, in fairness, had been obliged to admit he must be right. He felt extremely guilty about it, but on the other hand, try as he might, he couldn't sit or lie around in the room and be indifferent to it. Earl Hornick even whistled when his mouth was full of food. It had brought Mr. Clokey to the nervous point at which Mrs. McKee had found him—more or less compelled, that is, to find somebody like herself and get it off his chest. It revealed him to be a very weak man—as Earl Hornick had suggested—but to keep from going crazy he just had to discuss it with someone. If he hadn't found her to confide in, he said, he would have gone plain nuts.

Since he wasn't married, Mrs. McKee had pointed out that if he were it might have been different, as he would have been living with somebody who whistled, clicked their finger nails, or even worse. If he thought a little whistling was a problem, she said, he should pass almost a lifetime with a man, or a woman, who couldn't pass a living moment without something in his mouth. A cigar, a match, or something he would pick right off the street. He was like a child who didn't seem to know what he was doing, until you told him about it, or like Earl Hornick, the way he made a whistling sound sucking air through his teeth. There had been a time, she confided, when he almost picked her whisk brooms to pieces, after she had asked him never again to chew on a match. She had been as distracted as Mr. Clokey, not for three weeks but for several years running, until one day, hardly knowing why, she just didn't seem to care. He had gone back to matches, when he sensed that, and there he had stayed. All she could say now was that she still preferred matches to cigars.

Mr. Clokey had confessed that he himself had never married—although the opportunity had offered—due to a gastric disturbance he had as a young man, that followed all of his meals. Burping. Nothing he took seemed to quiet it. Rather than plague another person with something like that he had lived alone, when he might have married, and when the burping stopped he had other annoying habits, like peanut butter on fruit. If he had a fresh peach, or cantaloupe in the morning, he would eat peanut butter with it. Earl Hornick had complained of that their first morning in Mexico.

It had been a very strange conversation—they had eaten strawberries on a patio with a view of the mountains—and Mr. Clokey had permitted four different boys to shine his shoes. He couldn't bear to say no, and he didn't want to make little beggars out of them. In a perfectly casual and natural way he had suggested, if she could spare the time, that they motor to Oaxaca where he had reserved a pleasant suite of rooms. Earl Hornick, in spite of his art background, was so prudish he refused to travel with a lady, and

Mr. Clokey was sure she would never forget Mitla or the world's oldest tree. He hoped he didn't have to tell her that his affection was Platonic, and stopped at that.

The strange thing was she had not been taken aback, shocked to hear it, or anything whatsoever. It seemed a perfectly normal thing for him to proposition her like that. She was sure she would simply *love* Mitla, she had said, just from the little she had seen of it at Sanborn's, but with her grandson and her father to take care of, her hands were full. She had been tactful enough to leave it at just that. It had not been necessary—nor had it crossed her mind until she saw him, an hour later—that she had not referred to McKee as a problem, or anything else. She had felt precisely as Mr. Clokey had felt himself: that she was not attached to him in any serious way. That she was free to fool around—as he had said himself. They had parted on the best of terms—she had since had strawberries with him at Sanborn's—and spent some time in the lobby looking at the pictures he had taken.

What would Walter McKee, her husband, think of something like that? She was terribly afraid—no, she was more than afraid, she was absolutely sure, if he had been there, it would have been about the same as that incredible night on the porch. Not that Mr. Clokey was a Gordon Boyd, but if McKee had been there, and heard the question, he would have said "Lois, you know you can do about as you like."

Why hadn't she?

"Lois—" he had said to her, just before they had left, "you can count on the fingers of one hand"—and he held it up—"the people who know what it is they want."

As Mr. Clokey liked to say, *she would buy that.* What did she want? Anything she had ever had? In the windshield of the car she saw her face, expectant, the lips parted. What might have happened if Boyd had walked on the water? Would she have, that is? From her purse, the miniature bed warmer that contained her pills, her saccharine, and her aspirin, she took the pill that would help to quiet her down. Coming toward her with a paper cup of cold coffee, was McKee.

Scanlon

What the devil were they yelling? *Agua. Frijoles* was beans. *Agua* was water. But where the devil was the water? In the pit before him, glowing like it was hot, there wasn't any water at all. It was sand. What sort of fool would look for water in a place like that? Well, he could tell you. An eastern sort of fool like this man Boyd, or an even bigger fool like Scanlon himself. His father, that is. His father, Timothy Scanlon, had come from the East. The East was where a man went down to look for water. In the West, he went up.

"I tell you where we looked for water?" he said, but the boy, fizzing pop, didn't hear him. As if he didn't know better he was squirting that pop into his mouth. Another thing that eastern fellow, Boyd, had done to him.

"*Agua!*" he heard them holler, and he would like to tell them that if what they wanted was water, and not this Pepsi-Cola, the place they had to look for it was up. They wouldn't find it, but that was where they would have to look. If they went up a canyon far enough they might see where it had been. See where it had coursed, when the canyon flooded, and then see where it came to an end. Where the sun had sucked it up, or the sand had sucked it underground. In that valley they crossed there were round-topped buttes, spread around like so many Indian baskets, but there was never any Indian or any living thing to

127

shoot. The only thing in creation he could have shot with his gun would have been himself.

All he did, day and night, was scout for water, and he might be gone two, three days at a time. He'd carry that fool gun, a cup or two of water, a small slab of dried meat in his pocket, and after dark, up on one of them buttes, he'd build himself a fire. He'd eat what little he had, then he'd roll up his blanket, put his canteen at the head or foot, then go back and hide in the dark until the fire died down. But nothing ever happened. No Indian ever came to see who he was. No animal or bird ever snooped around for something to eat. It made him kind of careless, that sort of country, and if there had been any Indians in it, or anything that was hungry, he might have gone off and never come back. But the only living thing to hunt and eat in that country was himself.

From the high places he could see the wagons and the teams away back where he'd left them, crawling along so slow they always looked to be in about the same place. He found it hard to believe that the wagons he saw were full of live people, real men, women and children, who had left a home with food and water on the table, grass in the yard, trees for shade, rain in the morning if you prayed for it at night, just to come to a godforsaken hole like that. All these people really wanted, if he troubled to ask them, was exactly what it was they left behind them, even less than they had left if you could believe what they said. Every night Mr. Samuels liked to explain how much he liked to make the chips for his own shingles, and how they would stick, almost forever, once he nailed them down. Every night Reverend Tennant would read to his kids how they should sit and eat with the knife and fork, while they were scrounging around like coyotes for what bones there were left. This little Orville of his would pick in the manure the cattle had dropped.

From the butte tops he could see almost forever, but that was all he saw. It looked just about as empty, everywhere, except that to the west it looked even worse. He could see the slopes and hollows where even greasewood didn't grow. Way off to the south, round and shiny as eggs, he could see the bright shimmer that looked like water, and once, far on the side of a mountain, he had seen smoke. Maybe a week's walk away. All he could do was sit and look at it.

At night, if he could see the campfires, he'd try and figure out the Samuels' wagon, since in that wagon, wrapped up in burlap, was the water keg. When he got back to camp there would be even less in it. One night it would be gone. He didn't believe everything he'd heard, but he had seen Mr. Baumann sit and look at Mrs. Criley, a woman with water on her knee, like he was sizing up a good hog. There would be fat all over, marrow in her bones, and water on her knee. There was no water on his own knee, but he had heard Mrs. Norton complain that he wouldn't be so stringy if he didn't scout around so much. Stringy was the word Mrs. Norton used every time she put a bite of jerked meat in her mouth, and he knew that what she had in mind was him. He was too stringy already. She didn't want what little was left of him to get too tough.

He'd seen a flat-topped butte about a day's hike south, higher than most since it had juniper on it, and he headed for this peak so he could get a good look to the west. Along about noon, when he stopped to rest, he lay down with his head beneath a little greasewood, and on the branch right over his head he hung his hat. In the shadow that his hat made, he put his head. He'd seen the Indians do that with their arrows when they were in a country without any shadows, sticking the points of their arrows in the sand and their heads in the shadows the feathers cast. He took a bite of his food, a little sip of his water, then he took a little nap till the *thing* woke him up.

It wasn't the noise he made, for he didn't make any noise. He didn't fan the air, or flap his wings, but he came over so close, and it was so hot, that lying there on his back like he was, he caught the smell. Like a whiff of garbage, that was what it was. He probably didn't smell any too well himself, not ripe, anyhow, since the bird went off, and when Scanlon rolled over he noticed right beside him this small hole. All around it, like a string of beads, were these little pointed rocks, like they'd crawled out of it. They were alike in that they each had six smooth sides, and sharp points at each end. One was nearly as thick as his little finger, and one was so small he could hardly pick it up. They were all smooth and shiny as gems. He couldn't eat little rocks, or drink them, but it seemed to him they signified something, as if the Devil, down there in his hole, had got a little bored. He liked to tinker. He had all that space, and all that time on his hands. It was just another sign that he must be human, and evil as he was, with that awful smell, Scanlon couldn't help feeling a sort of shameful liking for him. Some streak in him was human. He did his best to hide it, but the rocks showed it up. If he crawled out of his hole he might even need food and water himself. Scanlon put the little rocks into his canteen, where they didn't turn to water or increase it any, but they raised the level so that it looked like he had more water than he did. Then he headed for this mountain peak to the south, and climbed to the top.

Hell itself, from the top of that mountain, lay at his feet. The sand was like ashes, and not even greasewood grew out of it. North and south he could see to doomsday, but to the west, where they were headed, he could see a mountain shaped like an anvil, glowing like it was hot. It looked like the pit where the Devil himself had hammered Hell out. All around it were clinkers, black as coal, but going off to the south, like a crack in a stove lid, he could see a canyon where water had once been. Clean white sand gleamed at the bottom of it. It seemed hard to believe that in such a dry place there had ever been that much water, cutting a canyon right through hell to let itself out. The only way out, once they were in, was to follow it.

When he got back to camp he fired off his gun to indicate that he had found something, but nobody ran forward to ask him what or greet him. One member of their party, Mr. Samuels, had shot himself. There was so little water left he couldn't bear to drink more of it. Reverend Tennant, as usual, had prayed for rain, but Mr. Criley had asked him right to his face why it was that the Lord, the one he prayed to, put a canteen on the back of a camel, but all he gave to a man out there in the desert was his thirst. Hearing that Mr. Samuels had crawled beneath his wagon and shot himself.

But he'd killed off more than just himself, and when they broke up camp, and headed for the canyon, the creak of the wagons made a mournful funereal sound. With that one shot he had killed off something in all of them. When Scanlon looked back and saw their little party strung out in the moonlight, the wagons ghostly, it crossed his mind they were already dead and entering Hell. And that the Devil had supplied them with just what they needed to get them there.

When they got to the canyon Scanlon went along the bottom, where there was nothing but the light, the heat, and rocks bigger than the wagons tossed around in crazy patterns as though some giant had been playing with them. The only tracks in the sand were his own, but when he came to a stop he could see his own shadow, smoking at the edges where the heat nibbled at it, and every now and then he saw this other shadow, the one with wings. It went around and around him, but when he looked up at the sky he didn't see anything. There was no croak, there wasn't any sort of smell, but every time he stopped this circle went around him like the web of a spider, or ripples on a pool.

So he didn't stop often till he found this place where the canyon opened out a little, with slopes they could get the wagons down all right, but they would never get them out. They would have to go along wherever it was the canyon went. He had a pretty good idea where that was but there was nothing he could do about it, and if it was Hell they were going to, he wanted a look at it. When he got back to the camp he told them what he had seen, without saying where he thought it led to, and during the night they spliced all their rope to let the wagons down.

They made a winch around a boulder, greasing it with fat where the rope would smoke a little, and they began with Mr. Samuels' empty wagon, and his two weak mules. Mr. Wesley handled his team, since he was young enough to jump if he had to, and the rest of them handled the rope at the top. The rope burned a little but even the mules got down all right. The men couldn't see Mr. Wesley but they could hear him hallooing to pull on the rope, which he had untied, and they pulled him up on the end of it. While it was still in good shape they put on the best wagon, with the women, the children and the water barrel in it, except for Miss Samantha who claimed she was strong enough to walk. They figured if they got that wagon down why then the worst of it would be over, but they went down the slope so easy there wasn't even a cloud of dust. The women waved from the back of the wagon, and except for the smell of the rope, smoking like a fat burn, it looked easy once they got the hang of it. So in the next wagon they put Mr. Fisher and what food they had left.

About half way down, with no more warning than the crack of a rifle somewhere behind you, the rope snapped right where it was smoking on the rock. They saw the wagon, as if the slope had kicked it, go up in the air and turn clean over, the canvas puffing out like a balloon, then fall on the team. Then they rolled along together, and they waited for the wind to blow off the dust. There hadn't been any noise, and it looked as far away as the wagon train from the top of a mountain, the canvas like a brown package all bound up with rope. Wagon, man and mules all wrapped up together in one winding sheet. Nobody yelled, and the only thing that moved was the cloud of dust, like a ghost in the canyon, with the ring around the package that was no darker than the ring around the moon. A shadowy circle, but it kept getting smaller like a marksman drawing a bead on the target, till there was no ring at all, just this bull's-eye on the winding sheet. And right when they all had this bead on it, a shot rang out. Scanlon could see that Miss Samantha had fired it, since she stood right there beside him, and when the bird dropped on the target he could see what she had hit. He didn't let out a croak, or flap a wing, and it was Mrs. Criley who picked him up, by his long red neck, and stood there picking the feathers off him.

It had been Mrs. Criley who used to complain when they ran the wagon wheels over a grave, but she held that bird by the neck like she'd lynched him, and the awful stink he had seemed to please her. Mrs. Baumann helped her pick him, and they both cleaned the skin off the quills with their teeth.

That night they built a fire, cooked the stinking bird on it but nobody troubled to thank the Lord for it, and a wind, as though a door had opened out, sucked out the fire. It didn't blow, it just began where they were camped and went off like a noise. Then a crazy-looking cloud went over so low they could see it scrape on the rim of the canyon, and a drop or two of rain, as wide apart as a wagon, fell on the sand. It left a dent you could walk up and see, but it wasn't wet. It scared him worse than no rain at all, and then a mule, without any reason, just up and went out like the fire, with Mrs. Baumann saying she could hear the spirit of him whooshing off. Mr. Wesley pointed out that it proved mules were smart. He had sense enough to die while he still felt as good as he did.

Scanlon wasn't scared to die—what scared him was that he wouldn't die soon enough. Off by himself where Mr. Baumann, for instance, couldn't dig him up. Where Mrs. Norton wouldn't suck out of his bones what little marrow he had. So he lied to them, saying that he would go on ahead, scouting for water, and when he got off by himself he just ran around like crazy, hooting like a kid. Just to be off where he could die by himself made him feel that good. And then— as if he'd come to that place where the door had opened, and the wind had rushed out—the canyon spread out the way a river does at the sea. And it looked like the sea, one of those dead ones, not shining white like the others, but black as a pit of coal when it was wet. But hot at it was, that place looked cold, like a chill when he had a bad fever, and it gave off a light the color of water that went up to the sky. It was as though he stood at the bottom of the sea and looked up through ice. There was no trail that led in or out, no stinky greasewood, no whiff of sage, no speck on the sky, and nothing in the air that he would call light. When he looked down there was no shadow at his feet. The sun came through a hole like you would burn with a poker, and the heat came in through the hole, and went out it, but this hole didn't rise like the sun, nor set. It just came and went, but he couldn't tell you how often it did it, or where it came from, or if you could say that it was up or down, or early or late. He couldn't tell you if he walked backwards or forwards, or to the right or the left. He couldn't tell you if he thought that was right or wrong. As a matter of fact, he didn't care, but the one thing he could tell you, if you asked him, was exactly where he was. He was in Hell. Knowing that, he didn't seem to mind it so much.

"*Agua! Agua!*" one of them hollered, and ran along the pit right there below him.

"In Hell there is no *agua*," he said. Soberly.

"*Agua! Agua!*" another one hollered.

"Shut your fool trap!" he croaked, but nobody had heard him. They went on yelling. Nobody cared. He leaned on the rail—he leaned forward far enough to see the crack in the fence boards, see it blur into focus—and where they were stained with the Pepsi-Cola he directed his spit. A bull's-eye. *Hmmmmphhh,* he said, and spit again. Then he drew a brown finger along the edge of his lips, as if wiping the blade of a knife, rubbed the juice between his fingers, held the moist tips to his nose. The smell revived him; lifting his eyes he gazed across the pit of hell, smoking with light, to the canyon where the downdraft, so cool he could taste it, made his edges uncurl. Dimly, on the burning sand, he saw the body of a man dead for some time.

"*Agua!*" he hollered, but of course it was too late. It was the wind that made the ghostly music that came from his mouth.

How did they put it?

The brave blood was the blood a man spilled first. Boyd could see it. Rose red, opening like a flower at the tear in his thigh. On the sober face neither pain nor shock, no indication that he knew, or feared to know, that this might be his last exit from the ring. All of that was on the faces of the two who bore him, one fat, one thin, like a sack between them. A torn, battered sack, splitting at the seams. Hero and meal ticket, the word made flesh, and the flesh made weak. Gored. The crumpled end of the hero's life.

"Imagine me being here," said a voice. "I've seen a man gored."

Another way should be found, Boyd was thinking, to bear him from the ring. It should be understood that he might not enter it again. Or if he did, it would not be as the same man. He would never spill the same red blood in the sand. They could do wonders, off where they would take him, the sulfa would do this, the knife would do that, and there would even be blood to replace the stuff that he'd spilled. Red, life-giving blood, but not the same. Brave blood could be spilled, but not transfused. One could see clearly how it was lost, but not how it was made. The brave ingredient did not show up in the blood-count smear. It escaped, like his breath, into thin air. It did not darken the sand, like the bull's, but like a dusty pollen, wind-borne from the wound, reappeared as a spot in the lung of some youth, a point of infection that would prove to be incurable. Nothing for him but to take the cure of fighting bulls himself. Sooner or later infecting, with his own spilled blood, the lungs of someone else.

They passed below: the youth's eyes were closed and on his forehead and cheek the golden sand of the bullring. Relaxed now. A beardless youth masquerading as a man. One who had put on the suit that called for the sword, and stabbed himself behind the arras. One who had dressed as young Washington, and saw the tree cut him down to size. Or one who—with that blood smear on his thigh—had cut through the line and hit one of the goal posts. A touchdown? No, he had dropped the ball. Very much the way a kid named Boyd had once dropped one in Omaha. The bull was now just a bull, and the hero was a youth named Da Silva, matador second class.

What had taken place?

"Well, it only serves him right," the voice replied, "if he didn't expect it, why in the world does he do it?"

A good question. To be answered affirmatively. In the expectation of the goring the hero was made. As well as broken. A crumpled top hat with the rabbit bleeding inside.

A matador named Salcedo, with the air of a man cleaning up after an operation, attracted the bull's attention, faced him like a camera, then went in with the sword cleanly over the horns. The bull *dispatched*. But had he *killed* this bull? No, he was already dead. He had merely added the finishing touch to the beef on the hoof.

The headlines would read DA SILVA GORED, the photograph show him froglike, as if leaping the horns, or crumpled like a broken toy as they carted him off. The camera did not lie. A pity, since the lie mirrored the truth. The camera would report what no pair of eyes present had seen. Not two, of the thirty thousand present, had seen the same thing.

Boyd glanced at the face of the child beside him, the pistol barrel in his mouth, his nose running, in his eyes the faint suggestion of the small fry who had overheard *something*. What had *he* seen? How long would it take him to puzzle it out? He was now a jigsaw loose in its box, the bullfight one of the scarlet pieces, but he would not know its meaning until the pattern itself appeared. And that he would not *find*. No, not anywhere, since it did not exist. The pattern —what pattern it had—he would have to create. Make it out of something that looked for all the world like something else.

Did he know that? Was there anywhere he might go to learn?

First, he would have to sense that parts were missing, and then, somewhere along the way, that the curious pattern he saw emerging was himself. Everything else he had been given, in abundance, but that he lacked. It called for transformation. Out of so many given things, one thing that hadn't been given. His own life. An endless sequence of changes, a tireless shifting of the pieces, selecting some, discarding others, until the pattern—the imagined thing—began to emerge. Death would fix the outlines. Frame the picture as no man would ever see it himself.

The problem? In an age of How-to-do-it, the problem was how not. How *not* to be embalmed in a flannel pocket, how *not* to be frozen in a coonskin hat. How to live in spite of, not because of, something called character. To keep it open, to keep the puzzle puzzling, the pattern changing and alive.

The lineaments of *Paula* Kahler—Lehmann liked to say—had always been among the pieces in *Paul* Kahler's mind. One day, like the fission of matter, they would out.

But wasn't that precisely *character?* Boyd had asked.

The old man had blinked. He hadn't said yes or no. In his face the wide mouth had moved as if his tongue were cleaning his gums.

"Wot I min iss—" he had said, held up his hand as if to show the healing wound in his palm, then committed himself. "Each accordink to hiss nachur," he had said. "I min sudge nachur ass he shoult haf."

"Then you mean ripeness is all." Boyd had said.

"Thod iss wot I min," he had replied.

Boyd turned to look at him, an over-ripe old man with shiny lips, poor circulation, and a silver hip flask clasped in his mittened hands. On his mouth, however, a ridiculous smile, like the one on the face of the tiger, the flavor of the canary still moist on his lips. Was he getting senile? He had the simple-minded look. Not unlike—Boyd was thinking—the trancelike face beside him, and in that face he saw the reason for it. They had grown to look alike. An impossible thing, but they were *working* at it. A transformation, a blending of natures often observed in dogs and masters, in lovers, and in the dual nature of a man himself.

Did Lehmann feel it himself? He put up his red hands, knowing what a sight they made in a bullring, and clapped with a frenzy that brought beads of sweat to his face. His eyes closed, the Neanderthal forehead contour wrinkled to prevent erosion, and clapping like a fool. For what? A dead bull. Something he did knowing what a pain it gave to Boyd.

Boyd turned to watch the mules, their pom-poms wagging, drag the carcass of the bull on a tour of the ring while the crowd applauded, some near the exit rose to their feet. Music, wind-borne on the draft that sailed paper airplanes over the bullring, suddenly stopped—leaving a void that nothing filled. In the quiet Boyd could hear the drag of the carcass, the rattle of the chains. The left horn of the bull—the tip that had gored Da Silva—dipped into the ring sand and plowed a shallow furrow, the wave of sand rolling smoothly over the tip. Washing away what little trace of blood it had picked up.

"Can we go squirt pop now?" said the boy, and Boyd watched the whitewing, with his broom and shovel, sprinkle clean sand over the spot where the bull had died.

Lehmann

He watched the boy with the gait of a dancer, weightless as if he walked on water, the hips arrogantly forward, flick the cape as if to rid it of a few moths. He gazed, as if along a track of ants, to where the bull stood waiting, then he offered the cape like a towel to a bather who had lost her suit. The head and eyes cast down, an attitude of dignified respect. In the pause a voice that knew cried—

"*Agua! Agua!*" and the wind, cool on Lehmann's bald head, fanned out the cape the young man was holding, exposing his bowed legs. "*Agua! Agua!*"

As if rising from the dead, the old man named Scanlon tipped his head back, croaked, "*Agua?*" He looked around as if to see it, then said, "That's water? He thirsty?"

"Dey use vater to holt the cloth town," Lehmann said, and showed how with his hands.

"*Agua's* water, *frijoles* is beans," the old man said.

"*Agua! Agua!*" and the young man followed the advice. He walked, turning his back to the bull, to where one of his assistants, just a head and arm showing, reached over the fence to spill water from a jug on the cloth fanned out on the sand. Leaving spots, staining it dark the way Lehmann's mother, when he was a boy, would spit water from her mouth on the clothes she was ironing.

He closed his eyes, as if he might hear the hissing sound as the iron steamed it, or catch the smell, on the draft from the kitchen, of freshly scorched clothes. From where he slept in the front room on

the day bed Lehmann could hear the creak of the
board, when she leaned on the iron, and see her strong
legs through the transparent slip. His mother loved
to iron in her slip if the weather was hot. She would
fasten it up with pins at the back, so the cool draft
would blow on her legs, and his father would slap
her smartly on the bottom as he passed. A sad woman,
wife and helpmate to Saul Lehmann, a sad provider,
mother of Leopold Lehmann, a sad character.

"*Agua!*" they yelled, "*Agua! Agua!*" and Lehmann
remembered, he could smell, that is, the strong odor
of chlorine blowing through the door of the Larrabee
Y. The sound of the keys Mr. Shults stood swinging
on his chain.

"My wife—" Shults had said, raising the blind at his
window, "my wife, she thinks I'm crazy."

Lehmann had said nothing. He had felt a little mad
himself.

"That name in the phone book," Shults had continued, by way of explanation, "but I keep telling
her, Gladys, that's just where he might look."

"You min for himself?" Lehmann had asked, and
watched Mr. Shults pop a mint into his mouth. He
stood at the window of his office gazing at the street.

"If you're looking for someone—" Shults replied,
"if you've lost track, if you're just looking—"

"I zee—" said Lehmann, and nodded his head.

"Does it matter," Shults asked, "if you're looking
for yourself?" He had not put that question to Lehmann, but himself. "He was the kind that might," he
went on; "you'd have to know him. He was different.
He didn't just think of himself, like we do. He might
not know he was lost."

"Strancher thinks haf happent," Lehmann had said.

"Dr. Lehmann—" Shults had said, paused to grope
for words, then drew the blind half way as if the

light disturbed him. Beneath it Lehmann could see
the ice wagon that had pulled to the curb. Under the
wagon the sparrows had gathered, in the cool dripping
shade, to scratch and pick over the fresh manure. Lehmann could see the steam rise, like waves of heat.
Shults seemed to have forgotten what he meant to
say, so Lehmann had primed him—

"You were zayink?"

"Stranger things have happened," Mr. Shults said,
soberly. "Stranger things did." He continued to gaze
out the window as if stranger things were happening
before his eyes. He sighed, then said, "What it was I
suppose, was the personal loss. For me. He grew up in
the work. I had him slated for something here."

The word slated had jarred on Lehmann's ears.

"Thees wass Paul Kahler?" he asked, since he had
lost the thread, if there had been one.

"He was my right-hand man," Shults replied, and
held up his right hand, the fist clenched. "You should
have seen him in the lobby. With the tough ones.
Had them eating right out of his hands. He was so
small, you know, and so helpless—"

"Wot do you think wass his proplem?" Lehmann
asked.

"Problem?" Shults had replied. "*What* problem?"

Lehmann gathered he had stumbled on the wrong
word. He tried to think of the right one. None better
came to mind. "Wot I min iss—" he had begun.

"Nobody has told you?" said Mr. Shults.

Lehmann had been on the fence. How much, or
how little, should he have heard? "I know that he
wass fery vrail—" he said, playing it safe, but Mr. Shults
wagged his head like a tired man. He gazed at the
palms of his hands, then raised them to his face. "Wot
I min iss—" Lehmann had continued, "in a psycholot-
chical zense."

On Mr. Shults' round face appeared a curious mocking smile. He left it there, as if unaware of it, and then, stranger still, a sound burped from his lips. A kind of sad raspberry. A soft, vulgar, despairing sound, Something he had heard behind his back in the lobby many times. Through the window they could see the waves of heat that rose from the top of a parked sedan and made the street ripple as if it were reflected in a stream. The awning over the delicatessen window seemed to blow in a draft. As if he were feeling the heat himself, Mr. Shults had leaned over and switched on his fan, placing a weight on the loose papers on his desk. Although it stirred the air in the room, it seemed to leave a gap of silence between them, but Lehmann felt strangely at ease in it, as if there by himself. He was amused, in such a curious situation, by his own peace of mind. As if he had been drinking. What explained it? He had gone for some time without food. He had passed that curious hour or two in the hotel room. His mind seemed to be both at peace and alert, as if it were disembodied from the man who had come along with it, a valet of sorts. Shults seemed to feel some of that himself, as he opened a drawer in his desk, fumbled at the back, and took out a collapsible tin cup. He walked with it to a water cooler in the back of the room.

"Dr. Lehmann," he said, "can I bring you a drink?"

Lehmann had shaken his head, and Shults had taken a long drink himself. It seemed to revive him, he smiled and said, "He was the nicest boy we've ever had," then came back to the desk and put the tin cup away.

"Thees wass Paul?" Lehmann inquired.

"When Mrs. Kahler died, following the trouble—" he paused there, then added, "there was just Paul and his brothers."

"No girls in thees vamily?" Lehmann had asked.

"Just Paul and his brothers," Shults had replied, and they had waited till a streetcar passed, the bell clanging.

"If I coot zee a pichur—" Lehmann had said, and Shults had sorted the keys on his chain, with one of them opened the bottom drawer on his desk. He took out a small photograph that was framed. He gazed at it himself, then handed it to Lehmann. It showed a group of eight or ten boys in the woods at a summer camp. Some were dark skinned, some were light, but the boy who stood in the center was like a strange bug—Lehmann had reflected—in a pair of shorts. His legs were so thin he seemed to be suspended above the ground. The long narrow face, cocked to one side, wore a pair of shell-rimmed glasses in which the eyes, large to begin with, were like those of a fish. A simple-minded smile of brotherly love glowed on his face.

"His first summer at camp," Shults said, abstractedly, his eyes blinking as he thought of it. "The next year we made him a Counselor."

Behind the row of faces Lehmann could see the word VIKINGS painted above the door of one of the cabins, and beyond the cabins a small, weedy pond. Two boys, in a flat-bottomed boat, were out on it.

"Reading from left to right—" said Shults, who seemed to have memorized the picture, "you have Domiano, Deutsch, Guagliardo, then Paul—Paul was unusually thin that summer."

"I see him," said Lehmann; then, "How did he get alonk?"

The boy beside him, a dark-skinned number, was using his fingers to make an evil face.

"You'd have to know him," said Shults. "You'd just have to know him. Everybody wondered." He leaned over for another glimpse of the picture. "I suppose they just took him for granted. He was never any different. They just took him for queer."

"He looks a little on the simple side," Lehmann had said.

"I think most Saints do," Shults had replied, so matter-of-factly that Lehmann let it pass, then realized what he had heard. He raised his eyes to where Shults stood pointing, with a pencil he had found on his desk, at the picture of a simple-minded Saint on his wall. His hands were spread out before him, and around his head hovered many small birds. Gathered at his feet were many small creatures, some known to be friendly, others unfriendly, but for the moment at peace among themselves.

"If he *had* a problem," said Shults, "I suppose it was to get them to see him as *normal*. But he grew up around here, so they finally got used to it." That reminded him of something, for he added, "That first summer at camp was quite a problem. Bedbugs, you know, and we couldn't get him to kill anything."

Lehmann nodded, then said, "How did you handle it?"

"Handle?" Shults queried. "He taught them the teachings of Jesus Christ."

The flatness of the statement presented no openings. They both reflected on it.

"And the udder poys?" Lehmann inquired.

"They came back different," Shults replied, "than they went away."

Lehmann had glanced up to see if Shults was smiling, but he had turned away. Facing the window he had said, "Dr. Lehmann, what do you do with boys who think that Christ is a curse, and Lincoln the name of a park?"

Lehmann had not replied, wanting to know what Mr. Shults did with such boys, and he had watched him take a sheet of paper from the drawer of his desk. A yellow sheet with the faint green stripes like popcorn bags, covered with a large scrawl that showed through on both sides. "Listen to this—" Shults said, cleared his throat and began—

"—the ringworm is worse among the Friendly Indians—"

then paused to explain, "The Friendly Indians were not in Paul's cabin. Ten cabins at camp. But the Friendly Indians were one of ours." He continued—

"—worse among the Friendly Indians where Frankie Scire has it on his hands and face and Emanuel Guagliardo has it over one eye. After prayers Emanuel asked me if the salve I put on didn't kill the ringworm, and if it did kill the ringworm wasn't that killing something? I said yes, it did kill the ringworm, but that it was each according to his nature, and it was the nature of ringworm salve to kill ringworms. What was *his* nature? Emanuel asked. And I said it was *his* nature to ask questions, and it was my nature to put salve on ringworms and answer them. Then I said it was the nature of the bird to get the worm, the nature of the cat to get the bird, of the dog to get the cat, and the dogcatcher to get the dog, just as it was my nature not to get anything. He replied he never heard of a nature as silly as that. He said a nature like that would not last long enough to get the worm. I replied it wasn't any of my business how long my nature lasted, but to be what it was my nature wanted me to be. Then I slept all night, as that is also my nature, but it was his nature to lie awake and think about it, as it is the nature of little La Monica to wet his bed. I expect to have ringworm any day now myself."

When he had finished Shults returned the letter to his desk. The fan rattled the papers, and ouside, somewhere, a boy with a hoarse voice called another one a bastard. There was the sound of a scuffle. Their feet could be heard in the cinder yard.

"Let me tell you a story," Shults had said, as if the noise in the yard had led him to think of it. "One of our big problems is slot machines. The boys rob them. They make off with the money, the peanuts, and the gum. When Paul was here we had a boy named Guagliardo—the one he mentions in the letter—who headed the gang that specialized in slot machines. The first summer Paul was here they came into the lobby with a shirt full of coins. Ran to around forty or fifty dollars in pennies, I think. They came back here and got hold of Paul, took him down to the towel room with them, and there they asked him to divvy the money up. Twelve of them, and they wanted an equal cut of it. He did as they wanted, but he refused to take a cut himself. This boy Guagliardo never got over that. I don't think he cared about the principle of it, but he'd never seen a human being turn down money. He recognized it as a superior quality. He couldn't do it himself. Anyhow, he never got over it."

"They did nod laff at him?" Lehmann had asked.

"We all laughed at him," Shults replied. "Let God strike me dead, but I laughed at him myself. When you simply can't believe something, you laugh at it. Nobody believes in goodness. Goodness without recompense."

"Iss that nod the bower of efil?" Lehmann had put in. "That it iss nod so hart in wich to b'lief?"

Shults had paused to think about it.

"Dr. Lehmann—" he replied, soberly, "I used to think that evil was the great mystery. But I don't any more. Evil is not mysterious. The great mystery is goodness. It cannot be explained."

"But efil can destroy," Lehmann had replied, "efen if it iss nod so mysterious."

"But only goodness," Shults had answered, "can create."

"That iss somethink you know?" Lehmann had asked.

"It is something I believe," Shults had replied.

And then Lehmann had said, "Wot woot you gif to zee it with your own eyes?"

"I *have* seen it, Dr. Lehmann," he said, then saw

that that was not the answer. He waited, and Lehmann had said,

"Wot I do nod know iss the gootness. Wot I wonder iss if efil can make it too, no?"

"What are you saying?" Shults had said.

"Iss it nod somethink?" Lehmann had said, "to make a man into a voman?"

Mr. Shults had been standing. He let himself down in the chair at his desk.

"Wot I min iss—" Lehmann went on, "wass it gootness, or wass it efil?"

Mr. Shults had raised his hands to his face as if he might weep. Cupped in the palms of his hands, when he took them away, he seemed to see the mask of his face. With one of the keys on his chain he opened a file behind his desk. He removed a large envelope, said aloud—

"Kahler, Otto—case of," in the voice of a man who no longer felt much of anything. From the folder he took a clipping, glanced at the headline, then turned from Lehmann to face the window. "Just before Christmas we had this blizzard. Snow piled up in the streets. One night Otto Kahler, who worked in the freight yards, didn't get home. He drank, sometimes, and I suspected he had got drunk. But he didn't get home for Christmas, or New Year's. Paul spoke to me, and we got in touch with the police. Sometimes a drunk would be lost till the snow started to melt. He never came home, showed up at his work, and the police knew nothing about him. In April, that year, the drifts of snow began to melt." Shults returned the clipping to the folder, then said, matter-of-factly, "I suppose, Dr. Lehmann, you know how these things are done?"

Lehmann was not sure. "Done?" he had said.

"When you find a man dead in the street," said Shults. "Or almost dead, anyhow, someone has to pick him up. If he's dead, he has to be buried—if he is not . . ."

Lehmann felt his head nodding. "—One muss wade till the man hass died. Yes?" he said.

Shults agreed. As if his mouth felt dry, he carefully moistened his lips. "Dead bodies are a problem, Dr. Lehmann, since it costs money to bury them. But they are also worth money. There are people looking for them."

"Wot iss a goot pody worth?" Lehmann asked, to show his detachment.

Shults didn't seem to hear that. "There is the record of a sale, he continued, "of a body with the first joint missing, first finger, of the left hand. In the Kahler family this missing joint was quite a joke. When Otto Kahler put that finger to his ear it appeared to have entered his head." Shults paused to place his own hands, the palms up, on his desk. He did not speak for a moment, then said, "In May a medical student, who made such things a hobby, recognized the hand that he was dissecting. He put formaldehyde in his lunch pail and brought the hand to Mrs. Kahler for identification. Paul was there at the time. He left the house in the evening and was never seen again."

Lehmann had started to speak, but Mr. Shults, as if he saw in his face Lehmann's question, slowly shook his head, a smile forming on his dry lips. They would speak the words, Lehmann knew, that he usually reserved for himself.

"The faith that moves mountains, Dr. Lehmann—" he said, then remembered the twist that this faith had taken. "Such a faith finds it simple to change the nature of man."

As if that statement had changed his own, reviving him, restoring his purpose, he rose from the desk and took long, springy strides toward the door. His hand on the knob he turned and said, "I can't tell you what this means to me, Dr. Lehmann. I have kept the faith for fifteen years, and now I find it confirmed."

He had kept the faith, and with Lehmann's elbow cupped in his palm, as if he thought he might falter, he walked him down the hall to the door where he had come in. As they crossed the lobby a billiard ball shot across the floor. Mr. Shults let it roll, a warm smile on his face. He beamed at the little thug who had thrown it, his eyes sightless with Paula Kahler's luminous gaze.

Lehmann did not wait, he made for the stairs, but before the door had swung shut behind him he heard the voice, disembodied, repeating the formula. *The ball is not may ball, Vito*—it was saying—*the floor is not my floor*, but at that point the creaking door mercifully closed. Lehmann looked up to see the lights coming on in the neon wilderness.

"*Agua! Agua!*" they were yelling, and over the ring, buoyant on the draft that twirled it slowly, like a dancer, a burning newspaper dipped and soared, like a ship afire at sea. Matadors, *peones*, cameramen and policemen, the thirty thousand who had paid as well as those who hadn't, turned their eyes from the bull to watch the sparks fly upward, skittish on the draft. His own face tipped upward, Lehmann felt the prick of blowing sand on his face.

"*Agua! Agua!*" they yelled, and then the voice of Boyd, as if closing the invocation—

"*Agua, agua,* everywhere, but not a drop to drink."

Lehmann turned to see him take the Pepsi bottle he was holding, give it a violent shake.

"So you want to squirt pop, eh?" he said to the boy, and as it hissed on his thumb, blowing a froth of bubbles, the boy pumped his small head up and down. Wagging the white-tipped tail, said to be a real one, of his coonskin hat.

She pressed the button to run the window down, and he passed her the coffee.

McKee　"It's what they gave me when I asked for coffee," he said, and smiled, to indicate it was a joke. She didn't smile, and he said, "If you want the heater on, what you do is start up the motor. Knob right there alongside the heater is the radio." She didn't bite at that, so he said, "Lois, that boy's safer in there with the old man than he is in the bathroom of your own house." The window she had run down for the coffee, she now ran up.

McKee couldn't understand a woman—women, that is—who couldn't bear to let a child out of their sight, but who had a bathroom with enough pills to put half the state to sleep. Or like the Cronins, these friends of theirs, scared to death of this polio business, but wouldn't blink an eye when the youngster drank the water in a cocktail glass. McKee had watched the little devil, time and again, scoot around the room like a vacuum cleaner, finishing off whatever he happened to find in any glass on the floor. "Probably do him good," Mr. Cronin had said, when McKee pointed it out.

"If they don't want to come," McKee said through the window, "I may have to sit there till the business is over."

If she didn't like that, she could always say she hadn't heard what he'd said. With the palm of his hand—a Mexican boy in Monterey had showed him that one—McKee rubbed the finger marks off the glass. In-

side the car it was dark. He hadn't yet puzzled out
where the light switch was. Reflected in the windshield were the lights from the fires in the shadow of
the bullring. *Barbecue.* It smelled good, but he didn't
dare offer her any of it. Never tell what piece of it
she'd get, or what animal it was. Might be that little
bull Boyd had squirted with the Pepsi-Cola, or the
big one that had tossed that boy like a sack. Made him
think of Boyd. The way he had the beginner's sort of
luck.

Anything in a circle, like a ball park, or those motor-
cycle bowls at the Fair, McKee liked to walk around
since they always brought him back where he started
from. He would walk a lot more if there were more
ways of doing that. But back in Lincoln, if he walked
around the block the neighbors thought he was sick
and just getting up, but if he walked in one direction
he ended up clear to hell and gone.

He stopped to watch a dog, a cur with hatpin eyes,
put his head down in a hole for a drink of water. He'd
seen a little bantam rooster, in a place called San
something, chase a dog like that. And yet the same
fool dog would have the nerve to stick his head into
a hole. Led McKee to think of the time he had done
just that himself. Stuck his head into a hole and all but
had it chopped right off.

Naming his firstborn Gordon—when McKee thought
of that he wondered how he could have been so
crazy, so soft in the head, as to have done a thing
like that. Came within an inch, God knows, of ruin-
ing his life. His mother wouldn't call him by that
name, or very much else. That worked out all right
for her, but the boy grew up with the idea that he
was one thing to his daddy, and another to his Mom.
What trouble they had with the boy, which was
plenty, could probably be laid to the fact that right
from the first he didn't really know *who* he was. It

took him a little better than eighteen years to find out.

One reason it took so long, in McKee's opinion, was due to what happened while the boy was still a youngster. It wasn't only women who could have their intuitions, and McKee realized, when he saw Boyd that Christmas, that he would probably never turn up with a family of his own. The fact was, he never did. Much as women fell for him, there he was all by himself. The name of Gordon on other people's kids, instead of his own.

He'd always had that crazy wild streak in him—taking that ballplayer's pocket was typical of him—and it had been just like him to turn up out of nowhere at Christmas time. They hadn't seen or heard of him for eight or nine years. Gordon had been eleven, going on twelve, they had this big tree lit up in the house, although it might have been toward New Year's since most of the needles had fallen off. Right out of the blue—McKee had been down at the office—Boyd called him up. McKee could have said he was awfully busy, since he was, and it was around Christmas, but he wanted Boyd to see how far he'd come along, especially his new house. Things were really looking up; he'd bought that little Maxwell with the California top, and he wanted Boyd to see how much the kids had grown. Then too, Mrs. McKee was looking better herself, with the kids over the worst part, and the time he had seen her while she was still carrying Seward had stuck in her craw. So McKee had picked him up and driven him out to the house. Along the way he stopped to pick up a pie, since it would catch Mrs. McKee on short notice, and he and Boyd had sat out in front of the bakery and talked a bit. That is, McKee had talked, and Boyd had just listened, which showed from which direction the wind was then blowing, since McKee, as a rule, never said a word. Any-

how, they'd just sat there, the motor running, and
McKee had got the feeling, hard to say why, that
Boyd had lost a lot of his bounce. He'd been taken
down a notch. A rug of some sort, as they say, had
been yanked from under him. McKee had guessed it
was probably some woman, but he felt so good about
the turn things had taken in his own life that he wanted
Boyd to feel more like that himself. Which was why
he said, just in passing, that the family would be so
glad to see him. Especially Gordon—he had said, then
waited to see the effect.

"Who?" Boyd had said, since McKee had never
told him he had named his son Gordon.

"Gordon," McKee had repeated, and sometimes he
wondered if he would have mentioned it at all if they'd
been anywhere but sitting there in the car, with the
motor running. Just the two of them, sealed off from
everybody else. McKee's eyes had watered, from the
way he felt, and Boyd had put out a hand and gripped
his shoulder, the way he had so often done when they
were kids. Then they drove over to the house, and
since it was Christmas there were red and green lights
over the streets in streamers, and the big evergreen in
the high school yard was all lit up. McKee had never
felt the spirit of Christmas, before or since, as he did
at that moment, and he sometimes wondered, until that
happened, if he'd known what it was.

When he pulled into the yard the kids were there
in the car lights, and Gordon had run ahead to open
up the garage. He was a big oversize kid like Boyd
himself had been. When McKee saw him there in the
lights—after what he had just been saying—he had the
damdest sort of feeling that maybe he had been right.
That the boy was *really* Gordon's after all. He was
only McKee's boy in the sense that he fed and clothed
him, kept an eye on him, but the time would come

when Gordon would bring him up. So he knew it. He sensed that even before the evening began.

All the boy really knew about Gordon was that they were having a guest for supper, since he didn't know his name, or that he had been named after him. And Boyd didn't give him any special favor, he treated them all like they were his kids, and had them laughing so hard Orien couldn't finish his pie à la mode. They just couldn't help it. Mrs. McKee had nearly died laughing herself.

After supper they all moved into the parlor where he let little Orien crawl all over him, the way kids of that age do when they like someone. Mrs. McKee had been proud of her parlor, but without her having to hint or say so, Boyd pointed out how much he liked everything. When they built the new house, to go along with it Alice Morple had given them this oil painting, which showed a lone wolf standing in the snow on a winter's night. The scene was Christmas, more than likely, as there were bright lights in the farmhouse windows, which gave you the feeling of how warm it was inside, and how cold it was out. They had that framed over the fireplace with a sheet of glass to protect it, and Boyd pointed out how much her own house was warm and cozy like that. It wasn't lost on her that he probably felt like the wolf himself.

Later they put Orien to bed, but as a special dispensation, since they saw Boyd so seldom, Mrs. McKee let Seward and Gordon stay up. Boyd had been almost everywhere since they had seen him, and McKee led the talk around to that, it being the sort of thing boys like to hear. He made it seem as though the Leaning Tower was right there in the room, about to fall on you. He didn't talk just to Gordon, but since Gordon was older, and in certain ways smarter, it was natural that he absorbed a little more of it. He got so wrapped up listening he didn't even notice his leg had gone to sleep. McKee did, since he could see his toes wiggling, as if they were wet inside of his shoes, but that boy was so smart he didn't want to let on that anything was wrong. In particular, that any part of him had fallen asleep.

They had traveled all over the world that night, and about ten thirty, when Seward got a little sleepy, Mrs. McKee had to tell them both that it was time for bed. McKee had felt sure that they would have trouble with Gordon, but he didn't make a peep. He seemed to be off in some of those far places where Boyd had been. Seward came forward, like a little man, and shook Boyd's hand, telling him good night, then Gordon had got up, and before they could stop him had thrown his arms around Boyd's neck. He had hugged him like crazy, kissed him two, three times, then turned and run off.

Right up till then there hadn't been a misfire. It had been out of this world. But when he hugged and kissed Boyd like that—something he had never done to his mother and father—Mrs. McKee had got as red as if Boyd had kissed her himself. As red, if not redder, than the time he did. After what McKee had been saying and thinking, it was such a strange thing that he felt a little spooky, as if he was a stranger of some sort in his own house. The boy had done it, McKee was sure, just the way that Boyd had once kissed his mother, because right at that point he simply couldn't help it, she had been so beautiful. He couldn't either. And he was just like Boyd in that respect.

But the damage was done. They all just sat there until Mrs. McKee put down her sewing, as if she suddenly felt sick, and got up and left the room. Then Boyd had hopped up, reached for his coat, and before he had it on was out on the porch, although he had come out with the intention of staying for the night. McKee had helped him get his other arm in the sleeve, where he could see the lining was torn out, then he went off without either of them having said anything. McKee had just stood there, the sky so bright and cold it was hard for him to look at it, and for four or five minutes he could hear the iron creak of Boyd's shoes in the snow. Like that wolf in the picture he had moved in close, then he had turned and run off.

Music—if that was what it was—led McKee to wheel around and look behind him. A whirring sound. At the front of a café called *La Casa de Usted*. On a raised platform near the entrance there were ten or twelve people, maybe more, some of them sitting, some standing, but all of them making this whirring noise. Mostly violins. But he could also see a row of boys with guitars. Two little girls, their long hair in braids, sat with something like zithers in their laps, plucking the strings with what looked like long steel finger nails. The noise was considerable. McKee listened, but seemed to miss the gist of it. He counted fourteen, all of them working away like so many little beavers, but without a living soul in the restaurant. Was it practice? All of them seemed to know their parts. But the only person who was listening was McKee himself. It sort of gave him the willies, like a movie he had seen years and years ago, when he was a boy, featuring an orchestra that was going down with a sinking ship. They had gone on playing to cheer up the dancers, but the dancers had all left, and then the orchestra had gone on playing just for themselves. That was how they looked, not scared at all, but resigned for what was in store, the little girls at the front aware of this as much as the rest. They looked, McKee thought, as if they had never been young. They were sad and resigned in the same way as the old. The noise they made was meant to be gay, full of string plucking and all kinds of whirring, but behind it all McKee could hear the life boats being lowered. They were going down, without a whimper, with the ship.

So was McKee. He stood rooted to the spot as if waiting for the floor to tip, the water to rise, when the noise, as suddenly as it began, whirred to a stop. There they sat as if the boat had sunk, and they had sunk with it. Would all be found in their places when the men with the diving helmets came along? It gave McKee the willies—he turned and went off not caring what direction, just to be going, and when he heard the roar in the air above him he began to run. They roared again. He caught the *ole*, which meant that he was missing something, but it had nothing to do with why he kept going, or the music he went on hearing, or the fact that he came within an ace of killing himself. Hit one of those cables they used to prop a pole up, went over on his face. Didn't kill him though, he got up the way that boy did in the bullring, thinking he was dead but surprised to find he wasn't, just light on his feet. He leaned there on the cable, catching his wind, and saw that he was almost back to where he'd started, and there across the street he could see the Terre Haute people talking to his wife. Funny what the sight of his own kind of people did to him. Cleared his head like seltzer; he calmed right down, and except for the sweat all over his body, and that bruise on his leg, he felt about as good as new. He lit the second of those two cigars he had bought, and without further mishap went around to the gate.

Mrs. McKee

She thought it must be planes—those you have to look ahead of the noise for—but just as she looked ahead, her forehead pressed to the windshield, she saw the lights come on. Up on the rim of the bullring. where the roar came from; but when she ran down the window to listen, the roar stopped.

Were the lights what they wanted? Had it got so dark in there they were yelling for lights? She could believe it—like people everywhere, they tried to get what they wanted by yelling for it. McKee among them. If she wasn't there with him he would yell himself hoarse.

It simply hadn't crossed her mind she would be leaving the boy where it might get dark. McKee would be there, but what good was McKee? He had been there—right there on the porch—the night everything had happened. That silly smile on his face. Bewitched even more than she had been herself. She *did* have a reason, after all. If Boyd had been to her what she was to McKee, and if he had then kissed Alice Morple, it would have been the last time he ever set foot on the Scanlon porch. Bewitched or not. She had said as much to Alice Morple who had smiled smugly, then said that she didn't see a person like Gordon Boyd wasting his time on a *porch*.

"What in the world do you mean?" she had replied. She knew perfectly well, but wanted to hear her say so. They were sleeping together on the screened-in porch at the back of the house.

"If you think you're *still* bewitched," Alice Morple had said, "I wouldn't sleep out here alone on this screened porch."

That had done it. In many ways it had done it more than the kiss. They were sleeping on that porch at the back of the house where Alice Morple, in her tomboy phase, had once shinnied up, and out in back was the lawn swing, painted white, and her sister's rabbit hutch full of big white rabbits she could see in the moonlight, and hear thumping the hutch. After that last remark she had pretended to sleep, but her mind had been in such a whirl that she couldn't. And yet she *had* dreamed. That much was certain, if nothing else. They were lying on this bed—the one they folded up and put in the basement over the winter—Alice Morple on the inside, she on the outside where the screens were hooked. When she was just a little girl she would unhook the screens and feed the squirrels that came to the roof.

So there they were—the sky so light it might have been almost dawn, but probably wasn't, because of the feeling she had that she had never before been up for so long. Then she had dozed off—there was no other explanation—and according to Alice Morple, who hadn't, she sat up in bed as though someone had called her name—and unhooked the screen. Alice Morple said she sat up and did it in a way that left *her* covered with duck bumps. She would have sworn there was someone on the roof, just waiting, that she couldn't see herself. That was Alice Morple, of course, prone as she was to exaggeration, but the fact was that somebody did unhook the screen. It wasn't likely Alice Morple, since the hook was far out of her reach. A disturbance like that, besides, would have waked them both. It had not been Alice Morple for the simple reason that Lois Scanlon knew she had done it herself. She had dreamed of doing just that, and that was what she did. She had done it when a man climbed to the roof—the roof of her dream, that is—said "Open up, sweetheart," and she had opened up. A moment later—just long enough later for the man who had spoken to have crawled through the window—the bed on which they were both sleeping collapsed. A simple statement of fact.

Fold-away beds do that all the time if they are put up badly, or have some extra weight on them, but they had already slept on that bed for two nights. Why then did it collapse? More weight had been added to it.

She couldn't say another body—there was no real proof that another body had been on the bed—but this weight had been there, and that had been enough. Did it seriously matter if all of that was described as a dream? In this dream the bed had broken down under the weight of what had come through the window—it did not break down, that is, *then* give birth to the dream. The dream began farther back, *away* back, but happily it ended when the bed collapsed. Otherwise—but never mind about *that*. Alice Morple had been lying right there beside her, and observed her sit up, as if she had heard a voice, and open the screen—and then the bed, mercifully, had collapsed.

Alice Morple had cried out—and both Roy and Agnes had come running down the hall, her Uncle Roy with a flashlight, but she did not speak when they called out her name, or flashed the light in her face. She seemed to be, they all said, in another world. Well, she was. She would have sworn it was Boyd, and not Alice Morple, there at her side. The foot of the bed had collapsed—where the screen flapped open—and her Uncle Roy had flashed his light on it, then leaned over and hooked it shut again. Alice Morple had been kind enough not to bring the matter up. The weight of the dream had collapsed that bed just the way it could be said that dreams weighed on people, bending them over till they broke under the weight—like the bed.

That much was known and witnessed. The rest she kept to herself. Alice Morple had been too flighty and jealous to be trusted with it.

When she read of those people at spiritualist meetings who weighed half again as much as or less than they should have, she knew in her mind that the scales were right, and the skeptics were wrong. She had once undergone such a change herself. Under the weight of a dream she had once collapsed a bed.

Was it any wonder that her feet, at the time, hadn't been on the ground? Where *was* the ground? What were the plain facts? One fact was, the plainest of all, that a girl could be swept off her feet, and in the plainest sort of way never be quite the same again. If McKee hadn't been there—"Honey," Alice had said, "no bed is going to collapse with *him* in it"—if McKee hadn't been there she might have settled for anything. Any Tom, Dick or Harry before she did something queerer than unhook the screen. Or before something more substantial than a dream collapsed her bed. Somewhere she had once read in the *Reader's Digest* of girls who thought that a kiss might give them a baby—but it was not at all as silly or as strange as some people seemed to think. Not if one of them had been kissed by a man like Boyd. And this kiss followed up by a dream that would collapse a bed.

If they pooh-poohed that, and some people surely would, take the boy that McKee himself had fathered, but was no more like him than if he had been the son of the moon. If he was like any human on earth, it was Gordon Boyd. Being his mother she was not free to say if the effect he produced on other women was like that, but the moment his eyes were there on *her* level, it seemed the same. When he acted in that play Boyd himself had written, and tried to walk on the water, there were girls in the audience who *swooned* when they heard he had drowned. Nobody needed to tell her what the dreams of some of those girls were like. Or of the beds that collapsed. Wasn't it possible that the bed was right? That it knew, just the way she did, and just the way that McKee himself did; otherwise would he have acted like a madman and given the child *his* name. *Gordon.* The name of his first-born son. Anybody would think that he had been having stranger dreams than her own.

And then when they had—according to McKee— finally straightened out their boy, Gordon—what did he do when his own son came along? Make an end of it? Not on your life. The first child had been born within the year, and Gordon was his name.

There would never be an end of it—there would be this new Gordon, he would have others, and they would have Gordons, all of them like him, all of them the same in the sense that you would never put an end to it. She hadn't. McKee hadn't. And now their own son had come up with this new one. The Scanlon jaw—she could speak for that, and the eyes wide apart in his face—but it was neither Scanlon nor McKee who looked out of them. It was Boyd. They would never put an end to a look like that.

One day—and it would not be too long, not the way he was growing and customs were changing—one day he would kiss a girl and the props in her life would collapse. Jittery and bewitched, she might even marry him. Not that it mattered. The crazy dream would weigh her down. She would unhook the screen, or if she didn't she would marry McKee, a pollen-bearer, and the first-born son wouldn't look like one of his own. No reason it should. Gordon would be his name.

The tapping—she almost made a face, McKee *always* tapped at her; but there at the window was Mrs. Leon Ordway, of Terre Haute. She ran the window down and Mrs. Ordway said—

"Now if that wasn't smart. To come here and just *sit*. Now if that wasn't smart."

"If we hadn't done that climbing, yesterday—" she replied, as Mrs. Ordway had taken the pyramid excursion with her. But she hadn't climbed. *When I get up like that*, she had said, *it makes me want to jump.*

"Well, you've seen it, anyhow," said Mr. Ordway.

"Is it nearly over?" she asked.

"They go on till they kill everything and everybody," said Mrs. Ordway. Mr. Ordway turned, his head cocked, to hear the swelling roar.

"Sounds like another touchdown, Irene," he said, just the way McKee would have said it.

"I thought you came down here to get away from that?" Mrs. Ordway replied.

The roar came again.

"Kicked the goal, too," Mr. Ordway said.

Scanlon

What did they want now? He could hear them yelling for it. On the sand before him, cold but looking hot, was the light that cast no shadow, and up on the rim burned the sun that never set. He felt right at home. It was Hell, and they all might as well shut up.

It was Hell, all right, since he didn't leave a track, just a greasy spot. When he put out his hand he could see the water in him drying out. But he didn't really care about that so much, or whether there was or wasn't any water, so much as he cared about what time it was. Had he been lost in Hell for a long time, or was it short? Since he couldn't tell the time, he had no way of knowing when he ought to give up. Where there was no time, how was he to know when he had done what he could? So he just wandered around—he couldn't say if he did it for a short time, or a long one —until he stumbled on this body lying in the sand. The body of a man. One who had been dead for some time. But dead as he was, a ghostly music came out of his mouth. It was the wind that made it, he didn't, and it was a wild hollow sound, like a shell, as if it curled around and around in his head before it came out. When Scanlon tapped on his shoulder he could hear him rattle like peas in a gourd. There was just enough wind to give him this voice, make a faraway music in his mouth, and stir the crisp yellow hairs on his head. Scanlon had the feeling he had seen him somewhere, and he had. The crisp yellow beard was his own. The dead man was himself.

166

Was it possible? To tell the truth, he had suspected it. There were two men within him, and he knew for sure that one of them had died. The better man? The one who had survived would agree to that. The dead man had died because he knew where he was, and had died of it. There was no grease in him now, nor water on his knee, nor lean stringy meat for Mrs. Norton, but Scanlon could see that the dead man had left his mark. The tracks he had made in Hell were not just grease spots. They had come in and stopped where he did. They didn't go out. But it was not the same sort of Hell, with tracks in it, anymore than Scanlon was the same sort of man, now that he knew who had died, and what time it was.

Was he crazy with the heat? It didn't seem to really matter, in case he was. He took a good look at the dead man, his better self, who not only knew where he was, but died from it, then he went off in the tracks the dead man had left in the sand. These tracks went up the canyon Scanlon had come down to where he found the wagons, right where he had left them, with the men still asleep around the dead fire. Until he woke them and said so, none of them had known that he had been away. Nor would any of them believe him, when he told them he had been to Hell. They said that he was worse than crazy. They said that what he meant to do was lead them into a trap. Mr. Baumann said he'd feared that from the first, since he was so young, and so much stronger than they were, and what he had in mind was to have Mrs. Norton all to himself. Mr. Criley said he knew that to be the truth, but that Mrs. Norton had nothing to fear since he and Mr. Baumann would protect her from a fate worse than death. They told her to put on what she wanted to save, and they would see that she got where she was going.

At one time Mrs. Norton had been so plump her

diamond rings were tight on her fingers, but she had got so skinny they rattled on her fingers when she ate. Her hands were so thin she managed to pull on five pairs of gloves. In the fingers of the gloves, as though her knuckles were broken, they could see all of her rings, the way her bony knees and shoulders stuck out in the dresses she wore. On her head were all her hats, piled up so high that her face, like everything else, looked like something that had been stored away in her trunk. All she could wear was one pair of shoes, but on her spindly legs she got all of her stockings, with the garters hanging down like fancy boot tops to her shoes. She didn't look real—there was so little but clothes that Mr. Baumann could lift her, weak as he was, like a little girl and set her on the back of the ox. Then they went off, with Mr. Baumann on one side, Mr. Criley on the other; but Scanlon had the feeling such a sight would freeze Hell over—if they got to it. They went off toward Hell, but seeing how it looked from the bottom of the canyon, they skirted around it, since the Devil didn't want them any more than the Lord. And the thing about Hell was that you had to go in, if what you wanted was out.

But he didn't talk about Heaven or Hell, except to himself. They had to be seen to be believed, and even after what he'd seen he still had his doubts. So all he said was that they had to go in, if what they wanted was out. They had gone off and left him with the women and children, an old ox named Brigham, and Reverend Tennant who was so weak he couldn't walk. He put the Reverend on the donkey, the older women and the kids on the ox, and he and Miss Samantha walked up front. He wasn't any too sure when they started they would reach Hell, but they did.

They got about half way—that is, they got to where that dead man should have been, but he wasn't—just a hole in the sand with the bottom of another man stick-

ing out. That man was Mr. Criley, what was left of
him since he had dug this hole in the sand, crawled
into it, then tried to pull the hole in after him. He
didn't answer when they called him, and they couldn't
budge him since he fit it like a cork. He made his own
wind, but the faraway music didn't come from his
mouth.

A little further on they found Mr. Baumann, who
had started a hole for himself, but he was still too fat,
thinned out though he was, to squeeze into it. He had
his snout into it, as if he smelled water, and the skin
had been worn from the ends of his fingers. In a pile
behind him were the rocks and sand that he'd thrown
up between his legs, like a dog.

A little further on they found what was left of the
ox. It wasn't much, since what little meat he had on
him had been chewed off. It didn't need to be cooked,
since the sun that never set had baked it right on his
bones, and he had been done to a turn while he was
alive, and just walking along.

A little further on they thought they could see the
big sleek cat that had eaten the ox, but it turned out
to be Mrs. Norton in h⸱r party dress. The velvet looked
as shiny and sleek as a panther in the sun. One of her
bony hands, with a glove still on it, had stringy bits
of ox meat stuck to it, and some of the hair, like a mustache, had dried to her upper lip. No one had taken
the rings from her fingers, the money from the purse
at her throat, or the gold from the extra teeth she had
brought along.

A lot farther on—but not so far they didn't make it—
they found water cupped in a rock, and one of those
little six sided stones at the bottom of it. And that evening, for the first time, it got cool and dark. The bolt
hole of a sun that wouldn't go down, went down, and
went out. But he said they had better go on, while it
was cool, and they kept moving through a night that

was longer, or maybe the word was shorter, than the day had been. When it grew light it wasn't off behind them, where they thought the sun should come up, but far up ahead, like a beacon, and they went toward it. They came out right smack on the trail they had once left. Then they got to Mountain Meadow, where there was food and water, and Reverend Tennant recovered enough to give thanks to the Lord for bringing them alive through the jaws of Hell.

That was how he described it, and Scanlon didn't feel like arguing with him. He had to be a little tactful, at that point, since he had to ask him for the hand of Samantha, and then turn right around and ask him to marry them. Which he did. He declared them man and wife. A little crazy with the heat, Scanlon may have got one or two things wrong, and not remembered others, but there was never any doubt in his mind about one thing.

"Boy—" he said, nudging the kid in the ribs, "what's the shortest way to where you're goin'?"

"To squirt pop, or to heaven?" replied the boy.

Scanlon didn't answer. He did not wag his head, nor blink his eyes.

"If you mean heaven," said the boy, seeing that he did, "the shortest way to it is straight through hell."

Scanlon said nothing. After a moment he said, "Hmmmmphh."

"I tell you—" said the boy, "about Davy Crockett?" Scanlon waited, and the boy sang—

> "He feared no man, he feared no beast,
> And hell itself he feared the least."

"And see you don't forget it," Scanlon croaked.

"Okay," said the boy.

"Slow it up," he said aloud, and closed his eyes.

A succession of *oles*, each one higher, like an object tossed in a blanket. But how slow it up? He opened his eyes and watched the bull make his charge. The man *Boyd* erect as a post, heels and calves together, his entire body exposed to the horns since he held the cloth in his left hand, the bull charging from the right. A pass called the *natural*. The most dangerous and beautiful. No ass wiggling, no fancy footwork, no sleight of hand with the cloth or cunning. A moment of grace when both man and bull were sure of themselves. The illusion of an irresistible force wheeling around an immovable object. A mere nothing. A man armed with a cloth.

What did it? What charm, craft or cunning dominated the bull? In his mind's eye—if he turned the flow backward, bull and cloth flowing away from one another—Boyd could see the still point where the dance was. The man rooted to it. From this point hung the cloth that blew in the draft, or quivered like flesh. The bull could understand movement, but not its absence, the man could understand both movement and its absence, and in controlling this impulse to move, the still point, he dominated the bull. Except for the still point there would be no dance. The cloth, not the sword, brought the bull to heel. The moment of truth was at that moment, and not at the kill.

Boyd glanced at Lehmann, the old man's forehead damp with the praise of perspiration. Fear and trembling, nervous indigestion, the attraction and repulsion of anticipation that a false movement would turn to boredom and fatigue. After the elevation, the drop. The orphic sense of premonition, of transformation, suddenly botched. The fever in the blood, the mood of excitement like the charged air in a jet's slip, suddenly stale as the fly-droning air at the back of a slaughter-house. The letdown. The sour prospect of murder in cold blood.

Ask the young man Da Silva, recently gored, or the bull Traguito, recently killed. So many words. But words had brought them together, and words indicated what had happened. Words wheeling around the still point, the dance, the way the bull wheeled around the bullfighter, the way the mind wheeled around the still point on the sand. Each man his own bullfighter, with his own center, a circle overlapped by countless other circles, like the pattern of expanding rings rain made on the surface of a pond. How many had been traced on the sand of the bullring that afternoon? Two at least. He turned to look at the non-still point at his side.

"Can we go now?" said the boy, and sniffled. Across his nose, from left to right, he dragged the sleeve of his Davy Crockett jerkin, leaving the mica-like trail of a snail on his cuff.

Back. That took Boyd back to the raw chapped smear under his own nose, the mackinaw with the crust of ice on the right-hand sleeve. *That* boy didn't sleep too well, when he sniffled, and in the room with the goiter oven he would gaze at the plain, white and rimless as a polar sea. Corn, in shocks like tepees, stood in the neighbor's field. The climate and the soil out there favored corn. So it was said. But the big crop, as the boy could tell you, was an easier one to harvest. The bumper crop was fiction and romance.

That was where the dance was. From that still point the mind rippled out.

"So you've had enough, eh?" Boyd said, and placed his hand on the coonskin hat. What sort of dance stirred beneath it? What sort of fizz was trying to squirt out? At the moment a miniature frontier hero, one of Disney's rubber-stamp midgets, chewing on the non-poisonous paint on the barrel of his gun. Any danger? No, the dangerous elements had been removed. From both the paint and the gun. It was safe, now, to chew on both of them. The way the coon had been removed from the coonskin hat, the way the Crockett had been removed from the frontier pants, the way Ty Cobb had been removed from the autographed baseballs, gloves and bats. These things were safe now. They wouldn't poison you, bite you, or fight back. The strangest transformation of all, that is, had taken place. The ends were all there—hats, pants, and baseballs —but deprived of their proper function. They did not transform the head they found beneath, they did not enlarge the heart. They were there, but they were no longer *possessed*. What had happened? The neatest trick of the week. All that one had to do to tame the bull was remove the risks. Along with the means, that is, the meaning dropped away from it. Instead of bulls, prime rib on the hoof; instead of Crockett, nurseries full of records; instead of frontiers, a national shortage of coonskin hats. The transformation to end all transformations had taken place. One had the object. One wondered what the hell to do with it.

"Kid—" said Boyd, giving a twist to the head, "how about me and you taking a walk on the water?"

"You don't walk on water," said the boy, soberly. "You *swim* in it."

Naturally. And if you don't swim, you stay clear of it. To eliminate the risks, you simply didn't run them.

You *were* something. You stopped this goddam hazardous business of *becoming* anything. Such as a failure. Or a bad example. Or something worse. You *were* rich, or you *were* famous, you were John D. Rockefeller without the oil empire, Davy Crockett without the Indians, and the movie starlet without the suicide. You eliminated, that is, the amateur. He ran the risks, he made all the errors, he forgot his lines and got the girls in trouble, and in every instance he lacked the professional touch. The object was to *be* the champ, not to *meet* him. That entailed risk.

Saliva—a flow of saliva the flavor of the gun barrel the boy was chewing—led Boyd to shake the pop bottle he was holding, take a swallow of it. Dead as well. The life had gone out of it.

"Don't it squirt?" the boy asked.

"It's deader—" Boyd said, and ruled out one comparison, sought for another. Looking at the boy's hat he said, "It's deader right now than that coonskin hat."

The boy wiped it from his head to look at it. Had he thought it was alive?

"It's a *real* one," he said. "It's not a phony."

"Is that so?" said Boyd. "How do you know?"

The boy stroked the real tail on it, and said, "It cost more. It cost four dollars."

"That's how you can tell?" said Boyd.

The boy did not answer. He didn't like the change of tone. He gazed at Boyd wondering in what way he was being used.

"When I buy your scalp for my belt," said Boyd, "will I know it's real by the wampum it costs me?"

He followed that. He combed his hand through his own thick patch of hair. Did it feel like *real* hair? Uh-huh. He looked it.

"How will I *know*," said Boyd, holding his advantage, "if it's *your* scalp, or your granpa's?"

The boy lowered his hand with a jerk, stroked the

tail of the hat. Did he detect some change? He seemed to. In the small head Boyd could hear the wheels at work. Had the word *scalp* he had used been a little too strong? Did it bring up some picture, some comic-book scene of men without scalps swapping them for coonskins? He looked worried.

"That was just a way of putting it," Boyd said, and gave his head a shake to break up the picture. But it stayed. He did not change the intensity of his gaze. The eyes did not question Boyd, or focus on him, but looked into his own as if to see behind them. Turning away, Boyd detected a change in himself. A big one. The real change-over in his life.

In New York he had often watched children, spied on them, that is, since it seemed to him that children, and only children, led passionate lives. The life, that is, that Boyd—once a prodigy of action—no longer lived himself. They struck out blindly, they laughed and cried, they cheated, hooted, looted and lied to one another, were cruel and loving, heartless and generous, at the same time. They represented the forces he felt submerged in life. All the powers that convention concealed, the way the paving concealed the wires in the street, the sewage and the waste, were made visible. The flow of current that kept the city going, the wheels turning, the lights burning, and the desires that made peace impossible in the world.

But what had troubled Boyd was not what he saw, but that what he felt struck him as beautiful. Was it possible? Like the bullfight, he kept coming back to it. What he saw might be vulgar or cruel, botched like the amateur's kill in the bullring, but the passion behind it, the force in the blow, the absurd risks, the belief in lost causes, had in it something that struck him as beautiful. What was it? Until he saw a bullfight, he didn't know. There he saw that the running of the small fry was the first running of the bulls. Every day

a fresh collection of gorings, heroes, and the burial of
the dead. The kindly matron who would faint at the
mention of a bullfight, would sit at Boyd's side, beaming like Paula Kahler, and watch the small fry strew
gore on the battlefield.

Had that been all? No, he might have made his
peace with that. But one day, on a bench near the
playground, he dozed off. When he awoke the bullring was empty, the swings and teeter-totters idle, but
a small child leaned against the heavy wire fence, her
eyes to one of the holes. So absorbed with what she
saw, or what she thought she saw, she gazed into
Boyd's face as if he were blind. As if she could see
into his eyes, but he could not see out of them. He felt
himself—some self—in the midst of a wakeful dream.
Had he dozed off with his own eyes wide open, seeing
nothing? Had this child stood there for some time,
gazing in? This child—for that was all she was, a soiled-
faced, staring little monkey—seemed to have seen in
him what Boyd could not see himself. What she saw
moved her to pity. Pity seemed to be all she felt. But
what *Boyd* saw, and what *he* felt, was something else.
He could not seem to close the eyes that she stood
gazing in. He could not speak to her, smile or wink,
or indicate to her that *he* was now present. He could
do nothing. If the child had run up the blind on his
true *self*, he could not run it down. He seemed to be
fixed, with his eyes wide open, a freshly mounted
trophy with the pupils of the eyes frozen open so the
passer-by could look in.

Had he been mad? For the length of that moment
he might have been. Or had he been—as he had come
to think—for once in his life sane. Able to see, at that
moment, from the other side. Behind appearances,
such as the one he made himself. Eagle Scout Boyd,
the pocket snatcher, turned inside out like a stocking,
so that the underside of the stitching showed. The

wing of madness had passed over Boyd so closely he had felt the cool fan of it on his forehead.

"Son—" Boyd said, but the boy had turned his gaze, if not his mind, to the pair in the bullring. The bull, drained of his purpose, the head low now, the tongue hanging like a clapper, stood like a man with his hands tied behind him, waiting for the *coup de grâce*. The matador stepped back, cocked his right knee like a trigger, sighted down the curved sword as down the barrel of a squirrel gun, holding at arm's length before him, so low it grazed the sand, the red cloth. He held the sword in his right, but it would be the left hand that killed the bull. If his eye followed the cloth, that is, the bull would kill himself. Which he did; man and bull flowing together, the curved sword disappeared into the bloody hump, and on that peak the youth pivoted out of the curve of the horns.

The bull? Boyd thought he looked astonished. He had the air of a man who did not know what had hit him. He looked around, now that it was gone, for the cloth. Where was it now? A water stained rag over the arm of the youth. Whatever life or magic it had, gone from it. And so it was, even as he stood wondering, with the bull. Cloth and bull, now that their work was done, empty of the power that had transformed them, at the moment that power had reached its highest pitch.

They watched the bull take one step forward, then drop. The matador stepped back, his right hand raised as in an attitude of benediction, and the bull, as if resting in the manger, his fore-legs folded catlike beneath him, looked pastoral. With the dagger used for the *coup de grâce* the peon sliced off one ear, then the other, and holding them like a torch the young hero began his tour of the ring.

Lehmann Wineskins, flowers, coats, hats and cigars were tossed into the bull-ring, like so many golden apples, the young man pausing to throw back a hat or a coat, keep a cigar. One of the wineskins he caught, held it over his head, and let the blood-red wine spill into his mouth. Bull's blood. White wine at such a moment unthinkable. He passed below, and on his beardless face, blood-smeared where his hand had swiped it, Lehmann saw the expression of a youth who had kicked the winning goal. Behind him, on the luminous sand, the body of the bull cast no shadow, and where he had bled one of the ring attendants tidied up. Shovel and broom. The enduring nature of the aftermath.

Once more the mules, once more the music, once more the slaughtered bull and feted hero, once more the horn and as the gates swung open, once more the bull. Dark as if he wore the cloak of a villain. Almost black. In the fading light one could hardly be sure whether it was man or beast. One could not be too careful. Dusk in the windy labyrinth.

One of the *peones* offered the cape and Lehmann watched the white horns, as if disembodied, make a scythelike cut through the air, a broomlike swish. He heard the scrape of sand when the bull skidded, dropped to his knees. Then the wind-born whoosh of the cape as it rose into the air again. Not unlike the drapes—were they yellow?—at the back of Lehmann's apartment, blowing in the draft when Paula Kahler opened the door. Blowing in, always in, from the

178

breeze off the East River, over Paula Kahler who liked to sleep in a draft. Over her body, that is, asleep and snoring, but not touching Paula Kahler. Where was she? She slept with wide-open eyes. It was only what she saw in her sleep that troubled her. Those luminous eyes, so serene in the light, flickered wildly at night as if the river draft fanned them, the whites showing like the moist knuckle of a bone. What did they see? They seemed to see the far country she had left. The lobby where the billiard balls rolled across the floor of her mind.

One moonlit night, awakened by her snoring, Lehmann had gone in to turn her on her side, but he had stopped in the doorway when he saw that her eyes were wide. She lay out like a corpse, her body wrapped in its winding sheet. The staring, sightless eyes had made him uneasy—he had the sensation that they must be drying, a film forming, like the isinglass film on the eyes of market fish. But he was still in the doorway when she suddenly cried out HELP!

There had been no mistaking the word, or the fact that she needed it. Gulped it out, as if choking, a last cry before going under, and he had felt that the corpse had spoken of the life beyond the grave. Needing *help*. So that both sides of life were the same. HELP WANTED was the big need in both of them. There was no trap door, no escape through a hole in the floor, or a door in the ceiling, on earth as it was in heaven and hell, a man needed help. This was his human condition. This was the basis of his brotherhood.

Lehmann had gone back to bed, but not to sleep, troubled with the need for help himself, wondering how many times, in his sleep, he had cried for it. It was a need shared by all men. No one was spared, no one was saved, none had a corner or a concrete shelter where the need of HELP would not one day raise its head. Each according to his nature—no matter what his nature—needed help. Saint Paula Kahler, who had changed one world, still burned with need in the world she had changed, and needed even more help in the new world, rather than less.

To the question, *Where was Paula Kahler?* a simple answer. Everywhere. Everywhere that any living thing needed help. Among those who knew it, like Lehmann and Shults, among those who feared it, like Boyd and the McKees, and among those who knew as little as the fly that had dropped on Lehmann's chest. Few would need it so badly they would change their nature for it, but all of them would one day advertise for it. Under HELP WANTED. Both the fly and Paula Kahler. One world they shared was that. One groggy fly was not much, he himself could be held lightly, but his need for help made him heavy. When he fell, as he had on Lehmann, it was with that added weight. An ounce added to the world's sum total of help-lessness. But the creature adding to it the most was not the fly, but Man himself.

The night that Lehmann and Boyd had come over from Toluca, driving late, through fog and rain in the mountains, they had come around a curve to see the lights of Mexico. Boyd had pulled the car to one side of the road. After two weeks of darkness, of lightless cities, the spectacle was not like those back where they had come from. It looked like magic. A bowl of light not made by man.

"You ever see a sight like that?" Boyd had asked, and Lehmann had said no, he hadn't, although, in a way of speaking, he once had. Not spread out in a valley like that, but trapped in his own head. The spectacle of the goings-on in his own mind. A laby-rinth of lights, perhaps millions of them, so that it beggared any description, flickering with the current of every sensation, the pulse of every thought. A milky way in a rhythmic, cosmic dance, evolving and dissolving, assembling and dissembling, a loom of light where each impulse left its mark, each thought its ornament, each sentiment its motif in the design. A simple human mind, not really his own since he had inherited most of it, like luggage, and had possibly worn out more of the linen than he had acquired. A mind that went back, that is, to the beginning, that in order to think had to begin at the beginning, since every living cell did what it had once done, and nothing more. It was *there*, then the word came, and it multiplied. In this manner the juices percolating in Lehmann, in the mind loaned to him that he tried to look after, had the same bit of froth on it that flecked the primordial ooze. So long as he lived and breathed he was connected, in a jeweled chain of being, with that first cell, and the inscrutable impulse it seemed to feel to multiply. On orders. Always on orders from below, or from above. The final cause erected the scaffold, ran the tubing up through the framework, then called a halt when something like Lehmann finally emerged. And in the bubble at the top, flickering with smog lights, this spectacle that taxed the imagination, that is, the luminous jelly that spread like a salve over the spectacle itself. Lights. Untold millions of flashing lights. In the suburbs of the mind, the roof brain, this activity was the greatest, a switchboard where countless connections were established, with or without calls.

The *thinking* organ? So one would suppose. But if that pipe line to the lower quarters was broken, if the cables with the wiring were severed, *all* thinking ceased. Everything was there as before, but nothing came out of it. Some connection with the *first* cell had been destroyed, the cable that carried the protozoic orders, the word from the past, and without this word there was no mind. It seemed to be that simple. There was no mind if the lines to the past were destroyed. If the mind, that is, was nothing but itself. A cybernetic marvel in which the current could not be turned on. There had to be connections, the impulse had to ooze its way through light years of wiring, *against* the current, since the current determined the direction. It established the odds. It was why Leopold Lehmann had emerged at all. Why he was as he was, criminal by nature, altruistic and egocentric by nature, merciless and pitiful by nature, but up there at the front of the bull, forked on his horns, as well as wagging his tail. In Leopold Lehmann the inscrutable impulse was reaching for the light. As it was in Paula Kahler. As it was in the species with the bubble at the top. But the thrust, even in reaching for the light, must come from behind. Out of the shoulders of the bull, on the horns of this dilemma, against the current that must always determine his direction, in reaching for more light man would have to risk such light as he had. It was why he needed help. It was why he had emerged as man. It was according to his nature that he was obliged to exceed himself.

"Why the hell *aren't* things as they seem?" Boyd had asked, and waved his hand at the valley of lights. Beneath them, as they knew, they would find a spectacle of a different sort. It seemed a good question. Lehmann had been slow to answer it. The flickering lights in his mind, once he closed his eyes, seemed to increase. Some of the darker corners of the world's sorrows appeared to light up. A rhythmic volley of questions and answers left tracers of light. The mind of Leopold Lehmann, the human switchboard, the man who re-established the broken connections—was he the one to throw light on why things were so seldom what they seemed?

And why weren't they?

They were not *meant* to be. They were meant to seem different—each according to the nature that was capable of seeing, behind the spectacle of lights, the constellation in his own roof brain. The universe in the process of being made. Each man his own, each universe unique, the darker reaches opaque with clouds of cosmic dust, or spectral in the light of old suns growing cold, new suns growing hot. Here and there in the mind's sky, without warning, exploding nova like Paula Kahler, lighting up the far reaches, the space curve ahead, the spine curve behind. Emerging and dissolving patterns of meaning, seeding the world's body with cosmic rays that each according to his nature would absorb, resist, or lightly dust off. Each according to his lights, such as they were, if and when they came on.

"*Luz!*" they were yelling. "Light! More light!" and when it came, high on the rim of the bowl, they stood and cheered for themselves, as if their yelling had brought it about.

"*Mehr licht,*" Lehmann said, softly, and let his arm rest on the back of Paula Kahler. Not till then did he notice that her head was on his shoulder, her eyes wide with troubled sleep. As was her custom at the bullfight, Paula Kahler had returned to Larrabee Street.

McKee

McKee had to bribe the man at the gate to let him back in. So many of these tourists were coming out, squeezing through this one little gate they had open, the man let him stand there till he waved this ten peso bill at him. Moment McKee did it, he knew he should have tried him first with a five. Paying to go back in after the best of it was over didn't make any sense.

The people coming out were mostly tourists McKee had seen in the *Reforma* lobby, respectable sort of people you wouldn't see at a bullfight more than once. The men with the women who knew they wouldn't like it, but had to see for themselves what they didn't like about it. A big fellow who looked to McKee like Boyd, one of the sloppier type of tourist, came up the ramp with a woman on his arm of about the same sort. McKee didn't often do it, but he turned to gawk at her. She wore high rocky heels, and her stockings had a black line all the way up. Made McKee think of that loft in New York where he and Roy had found the stockings looped around the doorknob. Same sort of man they'd found in it, same sort of woman who had left them there.

That kind of streak, call it wild if you want to, Boyd had had right from the beginning. He didn't learn it. As McKee could tell you, he was born with it.

Clear back when they were kids Boyd had found that hole beneath the Crete front porch, one big enough to crawl through, and they would sneak off there and sit in the soft hot dust, squirting pop. More than McKee, Boyd seemed to get quite a bang out of that. The reason was, as it turned out, Boyd had swiped the money for it from Mr. Crete's pants, since he could do as he pleased and had the run of the Crete house. Mr. Crete slept late on Sunday mornings, and Boyd would sneak into his room, while he was sleeping, and take some of the small change out of his pants. That took nerve. God knows what it was that made him think of it. He could have all the pop and Hershey bars he could eat just by asking Mrs. Crete for them, but it wasn't the same, the money she would give him and the money he could swipe. The pop tasted different to him than it did to McKee. He really didn't like pop unless he could drink it under the porch. All he liked to do was shake it till it fizzed, then squirt it in his mouth.

He had that streak, which was why they sent him off to school. The town of Polk, as Mrs. Crete liked to say, was too small for him. But Omaha didn't really suit him either, if you took into account the trouble he caused them, running wild at that ball game and tearing the pocket off the ballplayer's pants. And then a year or two later—in the summer, since he spent his summers in Polk—he had this crazy idea of walking on water, and made a stab at it.

They had always had this sandpit out west of town, but sandpits gave McKee the willies, both then and later, so he wouldn't have gone near it except for Boyd. But they had both been at loose ends that summer—it was in the fall that McKee had gone to Texas—and they had walked down the Burlington tracks to the sandpit to smoke some cubebs. They'd smoked, loafed around a bit, then Boyd had stood up and taken off his clothes, showing how much faster he'd grown up in most places than McKee.

"Going to take a little dip?" McKee had asked, since he just took it for granted Boyd could swim.

"Nope," Boyd had replied, "just a walk on the water"; then he had walked around the pit to a sort of platform, where they scooped out the sand. McKee had thought nothing of it—it was just the sort of talk he had picked up in Omaha, where kids were smarter, and since he didn't want to sound like a hick himself he hadn't replied. Boyd had stood there at the edge of the platform, taking deep breaths and then blowing them out, as if he expected to dive to the bottom and swim all the way across. Then he stopped, he just stood there, his eyes as straight ahead as a wooden Indian, and McKee had been so sure he could walk on water—or on air if he cared to—that he just waited for it.

Boyd had put out one foot—the day was so quiet the water had a smooth glassy surface—but it seemed a long time before his foot got to it, touched, and he dropped. No splash at all to speak of, he just dropped out of sight. His hands were flat at his side, like he was walking, and it seemed so long before he reappeared, before anything happened, McKee thought he must be just walking along on the bottom of it. That he would next see him walking up the beach on the opposite side. But he didn't—he popped right up at the hole he'd dropped into, as if he'd been down to the bottom of it and then pushed off. He couldn't swim a stroke, but there was not a peep out of him. He thrashed all around, like a wild man, and it was just pure luck he didn't drown before McKee, or help of some sort, got to him. But it wasn't McKee. What help he got was from providence. McKee knew that he would sooner drown than admit he had tried to walk on water and failed. If McKee had gone toward him he would have sunk and never come up. But he didn't drown, one way or another, but managed to get his hand on the platform, hang there awhile, then drag himself out more dead than alive. He just lay there sprawled out in the sun until he showed pink on parts of his body, and the sun brought him around the way it would a drowned fly. After a while he got up, put on his clothes, and back near Polk McKee asked him, like he meant it, where it was that he'd learned to swim. He could see it was the only way out. It was plain as day Boyd couldn't walk on water, but it was not so plain that he couldn't swim. Without batting an eye Boyd told him he'd learned to swim in Omaha.

One thing McKee didn't get around to ask him —since he figured it out for himself—was why, if he planned to walk on water, he'd taken off his clothes. But it wasn't that he knew in advance that he wouldn't, as you might think. That summer he was still wearing some of Ashley Crete's clothes, just to rough around in, and if he was going to walk on water, he wanted to do it all by himself. He didn't want some of the credit to go to Ashley, just in case he did.

That crazy wild streak in him—McKee went down the ramp to where they kept the bulls, leaned on the fence to look at them. Only two of them left. That meant he had missed three or four. That crazy wild streak in Boyd sometimes made him think the Cretes had done it, spoiling him with money. Or was it the crazy pattern of the town itself, which he'd often thought about but had never figured out until the time he spent all day up in the switch tower.

Not that he was up high—the top of the grain elevator was higher, and he could have seen even farther —but he had never sat all day in such a high place. Any number of times as a kid he had wondered why the streets in Polk seemed to run every which way, whereas down in Aurora, where his aunt lived, they were long and straight. From the tower, that day, he had puzzled it out.

Offhand that didn't seem to relate to Boyd, or to how he was feeling in general, but for the first time in his life he finally understood one thing: why in a town with so many fool kids he and Boyd seemed alone. You would think in a town of twelve hundred people what kids there were would all know each other, but they didn't, and that was the thing about Polk. There were hardly more than eleven hundred people, but there were two towns. There were four, that is, instead of two, sides to the tracks. There was the Burlington town, where McKee lived, and where the trains had bells and cowcatchers, then there was the Union Pacific town for people like Boyd and the Cretes. Over there trains had a long whistle and a caboose. If a train happened to stop, the engine was half a mile down the tracks. The caboose, or the people in the diner, was all you saw. But McKee lived on a railroad where the butterflies rode free to Marquette. The time McKee and his mother had gone to Aurora a big butterfly had gone right along with them, up and down the aisle, but when they stopped at Marquette he got off. Like he lived there. McKee still remembered that. When McKee used the word *railroad* that was what he meant. But over on the U.P., if the train did stop, the people who got on it had one-way tickets, and the people who got off usually got back on it again. On the Burlington the faraway places were an hour or so, like Norfolk and Aurora, but people only went if somebody died, then hurried right back. But Boyd often talked about Omaha and Cheyenne, Mrs. Crete spent all of her winters in Chicago, and Ashley Crete did nothing on a train but eat and sleep. It made a difference. But it took a long time to see what it was.

Forty years. McKee turned from the bull pen as if

he might see, down the ramp, back to his boyhood. It was only now, more than forty years later, that he saw why the bell on the Burlington engine went on clanging the way it did when the train had stopped. The crossing on the Burlington had no gates. The train came into town like a wagon, right on the flat, so slow that a boy could run along beside it and feel the hiss from the piston blowing hot on his legs. When the engine stopped the piston left a large wet place on the walk. The bell went on clanging even when it took water, the black-faced fireman scrambling over the tender, holding down the noisy chute, and sometimes taking a drink himself. Where the water dripped on the coal it was shiny black. In the winter it looked like a load of snow, and up front, around the hissing piston, icicles with the flavor of coal oil could be broken off.

Why weren't there any gates? Nobody crossed those tracks but Boyd and McKee. On their way, as McKee remembered, down the Burlington tracks to the switch tower, where the gypsy wagons, in the spring and summer, camped night after night. They unhitched their skinny horses and let their cattle crop the ditch grass. No matter which railroad you lived on, if you looked down the tracks you could see their fires at night. They didn't sing or dance to speak of, but they burned a lot of railroad ties. Boyd had told him that gypsies would kidnap white boys, drive off with them, and hold them for ransom, which was why they walked down to see them as often as they did. In the shade of the switch tower, where the tracks crossed, they would chew licorice and wait to be kidnapped. Not McKee, but he knew very well that Boyd did. He took McKee along so there would be proof of it.

That wild streak in his nature went on turning up the way weeds would, when you plowed them under,

till you honestly couldn't tell the weeds from the
corn. But that was years back. That was back when
he was full of corn. When he could make a woman
like Agnes Scanlon, who'd been married ten years,
just as skittish as a kitten, then turn and kiss a girl who
had never been kissed before. Mrs. McKee liked to
say that he would never in the world do that again.
McKee wasn't so sure. He didn't say so, naturally,
but he would bet you dollars to doughnuts that if
Boyd had gone back he'd have kissed both girls again.
If he'd gone right back, while it was still dark, he
would have kissed her all right. McKee knew all about
what her intuition told her, but there were times when
that was not much help. That was one of those times.
If McKee had been a girl, he would have kissed him
himself.

McKee wheeled around, hearing the roar, and took
a look up one of the tunnels. Was it paper they were
throwing? No, they were waving handkerchiefs. He
almost ran, not wanting to miss it, whatever it was.
Then the way it all fell away, like a funnel with that
hole at the bottom, made him so dizzy he had to stop
and close his eyes. Instead of letting up, the yelling
seemed to get worse. He opened his eyes and saw that
everybody, almost everybody was standing up, waving
whatever they had, or throwing it into the ring. Mc-
Kee could see the bull over near a funk hole, dead
now, looking as sorry and helpless as cows did when
he saw them lying down. But right there below, so
close to the fence McKee had to stretch a little to see
him, was the starry-eyed boy that everybody seemed
to be yelling for. He went along at a trot, holding in
one hand a bouquet of flowers somebody had thrown
him, and in the other, like it meant more to him,
something that looked like a purse. Had they thrown
him money? They wouldn't do it that way back in

the States. The youngsters got the money, too much
of it, but you'd never catch people throwing it at
them. On the other hand they didn't run the risks this
boy had just run. All along his front, and down one
pants leg, you could see the bull's blood. McKee felt
in himself a surge of the emotion they were all feeling,
that had got them to yelling, which he couldn't do
himself but he could blink his eyes and let his nose
run. It crossed his mind that that boy probably felt
the way Boyd might have felt if he had walked on
the water, really done it, instead of almost drowning.
He had never before seen it in just that light. It helped
explain the bullfight a little, and Boyd's interest in it.
He looked around for Boyd—all this excitement would
mean more to Boyd than it did to the others—but in
the general commotion, with everybody standing, it
was like that crazy afternoon at the ball park when
Boyd, with that dang foul ball, had gone over the
fence. But it was different in the sense that he had
dropped it. The bull had got him.

The boy went around twice, as though the applause
had gone to his head and made him a little silly, but
everybody seemed to understand that and make al-
lowance for it. Just to see a youngster as tickled as
that did all of them good. The second time around he
ducked into the funk hole, where he went along the
runway, waving to people, to where one of them
stopped him and offered him a hat. The young man
put it on his head, then passed it back. Everybody who
was close enough to see that laughed, but McKee,
dark as it was getting, couldn't see who it was until
they had settled back in their seats. That left Boyd
standing. On his head was the little fellow's coonskin
hat.

Mrs. McKee

Looking for aspirin, she went through her purse, then the pockets of the coat McKee had left in the seat, where she found one of the questionable post cards he mailed back to old friends. A drawing of two shabby horses, one of them plainly a male, with this wretched little colt shivering between them. It was captioned MAMA'S SLIP IS SHOWING, although nothing whatsoever was showing on the female. Nothing. She turned on the dashboard light to study it. She could hardly complain about his cards if the questionable point they made escaped her, but on the other hand nothing proved so well that they were questionable. It was addressed to Emil Cory, his barber, so she put it in her purse for further study, since all of the cards he received from his clients were posted on his mirror. It would not be through any slip of *hers* showing if this one was.

Looking—she went through the basket where they kept sunburn lotion, soda mint tablets, flint for the boy's sparkler guns, and McKee's box of kitchen matches—before she remembered that aspirin was out. She had been advised to go easy on aspirin. Looking for Bufferin she found the road maps and part of an Omaha paper in the glove drawer. Months old. Why had McKee hung on to it? She read the headlines, history at the time, of unforgettable events she had already forgotten, then she opened it and saw this picture of her father looking frozen to death, his feet in the oven, wrapped up in buffalo robes and wearing his cane-sided drayman's hat. The caption read—

MAN WHO KNEW BUFFALO BILL SPENDS LONELY XMAS

She remembered McKee's hoarse voice on the phone asking her if she had seen the Omaha paper, although he knew she never saw it unless he brought it home. Which he did, with that picture of her father and the piece about the frontiersmen, now forgotten, although their very own children were living well and happy in the same state. Some brakeman, one who had known her father, had found him in the kitchen with his fire out, his feet in the oven of the range where he insisted on keeping them. He had been too cold and too feeble to get up and start the fire. He had just sat there, hibernating, until this brakeman had found him, and a story as pitiful as that just naturally made news.

There had been nothing to say. Nothing.

Everybody in Lincoln knew her maiden name was Scanlon, and that this old man out in Lone Tree was her father, but they were ready to forget that they had always known he was mad as an owl. Then overnight was an old frontiersman. He knew Buffalo Bill. She had known Buffalo Bill herself, having been lifted from the ground to his saddle, and he was every bit as silly, as smelly, and as hopeless, as her father himself.

McKee had brought the paper home, and that very evening, even though they had their grandson, Gordon, there with them, they got into the car and drove the hundred eighty miles to Lone Tree. It proved to be a turning point in their lives—all of their lives, in some ways—that little Gordon just happened to be wearing his coonskin hat. McKee had bought the

Davy Crockett outfit for him for Christmas, and he had
just put it on.

Not that they knew that at the time; they knew
nothing, and by the time they got to Lone Tree, a
four-hour drive, she was sure that dozens of curious
sightseers would be there. Hadn't the article pointed
out how old and lonely he was? But there had not
been a soul, not a car in the town nor anybody who
cared in the Highway Diner, where they stopped for
coffee and in order to ask how things seemed to be.
The old man in the diner had not read the paper, or
heard anything. He said that so far as he knew Tom—
that was her father—was about the same as usual,
which was all right. So they had not said a word
about the Omaha paper, and drove the half mile into
town, if that was what you could call it, where her
father had been born in the covered wagon that could
still be seen behind the livery stable. The Lone Tree
too was still there, what was left of it, almost the
color of ice in the winter moonlight, but no light at
all could be seen in the hotel, until they waded
through the drifts to the back, where McKee had
seen a lamp. He had it on the floor beside him, with
a tin cup of coffee balanced on the top of the chimney,
to warm it, and around the rim of one of the stove lids
they could see the banked fire. McKee had knocked,
but when he got no answer he had stepped in. Her
father had been asleep. When they stepped in he
turned up the lamp and held it out before him, and
it just so happened, thanks be to God, that the light
fell on the boy. Her father asked him who *he* was, he
replied Davy Crockett, and that was that.

They could have driven home with him that night—
he would have done anything the boy suggested—but
McKee wanted to wait until it was light. He didn't
want to drive him clear to Lincoln, then bring him
back again. He wanted to see if the boy still had the

upper hand after he'd seen him in the light. So they spent that night in her father's hotel, where no one but her father had spent a night for years, and everything had been left as if the people had thought the place was on fire. There were hats on the rack that were not her father's, and rubbers in the hall. In the lobby all the chairs faced the window where the town would have been, if there had been one, the snow deep in the holes for the basements of the houses that had never been built. On the seat of a chair she found a Kansas City paper dated February, 1918, announcing that an armistice might be reached almost any day. The wall clock had stopped, perhaps the same year, and the safe with the painting of the mountain waterfall on the door still had the combination for the lock written in pencil on the floor. In the keyholes just above it were two or three keys, since the guests carried them in their pockets, and a letter for a man named Lyman Youngblood, mailed from Terre Haute. It had been postmarked in May, 1926.

Her father slept in the chair where they had found him, but she had gone upstairs to make up their own beds, and found them all, the twelve beds in the hotel, as if the guests had got out of them that morning, leaving the pillows rumpled, the sheets and covers thrown back.

Had her father, as the sheets got dirty, moved from room to room? Beginning up at the top where she had once left him, sick with something called erysipelas, propped in the bed with all of his clothes on, the hat on his shaved head, a night pot full of cigar butts on the floor at his side. That had been *his* room—the one on the west, looking down the stretch of track toward Ogallala and the crossing where the downgrade freights hit so many buggies and teams. In such an empty country, how was it possible? Where there had been so few teams, so few trains, why did they meet so often at that crossing, in plain daylight, where nothing blocked the view? It had made her doubt her own life. Doubt that she knew what she knew. That trains, coming down those tracks, had killed full grown men who preferred to walk there, their backs turned to the whistle, rather than walk in the cinders just to one side.

Why was that? It was one of the things her mother knew. If I'd stayed there, she had said, I'd have walked down the tracks myself. But her father had stayed. Some would have said that he killed himself without the trains.

But from his window, where there was nothing to see, he had seen many things. There had been Emil Bickel, a bearded man with a lovely wife, and everything to live for, swinging like a scarecrow from the telephone wires, the buttons gone from his vest. Popped, her father had said, by the force of it. He had been dressed for church, all of his bills were paid, and the gold watch in his pocket, the crystal unbroken, had stopped at exactly eleven seventeen. The fast eastbound mail train, rolling down the grade, had been two minutes late.

Her grandfather had built the hotel at a time when men were saying *Go west, young man, go west*—but the town itself, and the people who were born there, all went east. No house or store, no building of any kind, lay to the west. Her father's window looked out on a short spur of tracks, an abandoned cattle loader, a pile of tarred railroad ties, and then mile after mile, or so it seemed to her, of burned ditch grass. Smoke from this grass often darkened the sky. In the winter and spring this grass might be green, a fresh, winter-wheat color, but all she seemed to remember was the smell of burning yellow grass in her nose. It seemed to be trapped in the sky overhead, and in the rooms of the hotel. In the middle of the winter, stronger than the smell of food, it was there in the hall. Eastern women would complain to her mother that they feared it was a fire, and throw open the windows, but the fresh air never cleared it out. In the summer and fall more of it would just blow in.

By the time she had been old enough to wait on him, and run up the stairs with his food, her father had been known as *the man in the room.* In the bed, as a rule, fully clothed, propped up on a pillow so he could see out the window, or see in the mirror the body of the man stretched out on the bed. That was where she looked for him, herself. On his head this silly hat, with the drayman's license, the soft crown of the hat shaped to his skull, and the row of soiled matches in the strap at the front. Then his coat—her father was made up of parts, like the hotel, of what the guests had left in the rooms—a coat of black material, scratchy-looking, left to him by a desk clerk named Riddlemosher. Part of a patchwork quilt was usually drawn over his legs. He had complained, even way back then, of the cold in his feet and hands. But he had no face—no, this man, her father, who was alive and had a face for others—seemed to have nothing, for her, between his drayman's license and his coat. Just one of those blanks, spotted with little numbers, that she used to trace in with her pencil, the likeness always turning out to be different than she had thought.

When she thought of her father—and she often did—she saw *things.* The oil lamp, with its wick floating like something that would one day bite him, and the flour-sack towels with the design that would show up when he wiped his hands. Always speechless— when she saw dioramas, the old man in them was her father—dying in the bed, feathering the arrow, or standing at the screen to judge the weather. But never comment on it. Just judge it, as her mother said, and let it be damned.

She hadn't slept a wink all that night, the stale smell of the grass smoke was there in the room, and she remembered how the fire hose cart, when it came, had come without the hose. They had been scared to death the new hotel would burn down before the hose arrived. It had been a dry summer, bad for fires, and all the traveling salesmen smoked cigars in their rooms. The hotel didn't burn, but at the end of that summer her mother took all of her children and moved to Lincoln. She had sworn before she left him that the hose would never come, and it never did. Neither did the speculators who would build the town, the Zion that would bloom in the desert, nor the grass fire that would mercifully burn it all to the ground. Nothing had *ever* happened: exactly as her mother had said.

She remembered her mother, her skirts whipping around her, ringed in by a blowing line of wash, her jaw set on the clothespins in her mouth. All the clothespins had the deep marks of her teeth. They weren't chewed. Just marked where her teeth clamped down on them. She didn't like it outside; she liked it better in her kitchen, a slave to the sink, the mop and the stove, but where she could draw the one curtain at the window and not have to look out. She knew, without troubling to look, what she would see.

But in the evening she might sit in one of the rockers at the front of the lobby, facing the window, and look out at the town she knew would never go up. Rows of maples and elms, lights that would swing over the corners and trap the June bugs, and concrete sidewalks down which she would never walk. Down the tracks a crossing with a crossing bell, or the gates that dropped when a train came to keep men who didn't know better from killing themselves. Across the tracks big houses, spacious lawns, young women to bear and wash the children, old women to watch and love them, and a man to shovel snow from the walk, mow the lawns. Out in back would be grapes, growing over an arbor, a lawn swing stained with mulberries, and a woman like herself cutting flowers with a pair of shears.

That was what she saw, sitting in the rocker, but the view from the kitchen window showed a road where the tracks were tangled like mop strings, and never went anywhere. A picture of her husband, Thomas Scanlon, more dead than alive even before she had left him, but he had gone on to survive her by sixteen years. To see his picture in the paper, to find himself an old frontiersman, a friend of Buffalo Bill, and to spend the winter of his eighty-eighth year in Mexico. Reunited with his family, attending a bullfight with his great-grandson.

If there had been one reason she had to get away from home *this* Christmas, get away somewhere, it was that all of their friends, some of them wiseacres, would be around to ask her father if he liked *this* Christmas better than the last. And if she knew him at all, and she did, she knew what he would say. He would say no. So they were spending this Christmas somewhere else. She wouldn't care—when they asked him—if he liked Mexico or not.

She leaned forward, her face near the windshield, to peer at the dark curve of the bullring, where the lights made a soft glow on the sky. A cardboard cloud, small and unreal, like those puffs shells made in the silent movies, led her to stiffen a bit and sit waiting for the noise. It came, but it was made by the roar from the crowd. When it had passed she noticed the duck bumps on her arms.

If they should ask her how *she* liked it—it would depend who asked her, wouldn't it? If Alice Morple should ask her, and she would, she would first of all mention the oxygen hunger, the vertigo and the goose flesh, as well as what she had observed the Latin countries did to certain types of women, as well as men. No more. Let her guess what types she had in mind. Let her guess if it was all a dream, as it had once been, or if this time the bed had broken down under something else. Let her guess. The thing about Mexico was—and she would say so—that it had her guessing herself.

Howling like an Indian, the boy cried, "My hat! My hat!"

Boyd
"Okay, kiddo—" said Boyd, and took a good grip on him, as if he was a bottle, then clamped the coonskin on his head and screwed it on with a twist. The boy let out a yell, and Boyd said—

"There's your goddam hat. Now shut up."

Oddly enough, he did. His lower lip trembling. Unaccustomed as he was to that sort of treatment, language like that. Something he would remember? Boyd smiled. Had he given his namesake something to remember? The old fool at the bullfight who had cussed him and screwed his hat on his head.

"That hat feels better now," he said, "doesn't it?"

The boy felt it with his hand, then bit down on his lip.

"It's a real hat now," went on Boyd, "because it's been on the head of a hero. That makes it real."

Did it? He felt highly unreal himself. This time the clowning had let him down, rather than picked him up. He should have left before the hero. He should have kept his big mouth shut. He felt as listless and stale as the ex-bullfighter, the winded old man in the funk hole, whose arms seemed to hang from the padded shoulders of his coat. An ex-hero. Once something of a youth and hero himself. One could see that in his smile, stale as it was, and in the eyes now too big for the sockets, as his bottom was now too big for the pants. But once the praise had showered down on himself. More than once, perhaps, the red wine from the skin had spilled on his face. Flowers, cigars, and

201

the lips of young women had been his. One could see it, staled as it was by the blackened teeth, the popping eyes, and the arms that hung like the sleeves of an empty coat. Once a hero, the undulant fever remained in the blood. The hot moments of the funk hole followed by the chills of polar nights. Followed by nothing. Neither melancholy, madness, nor the consolations of despair.

"Touch bottom—" Boyd whispered, with just his lips, as a man crosses himself in the presence of the disaster, then turned to see the sorrowful eyes of Lehmann pitying him. Eyes that knew. Boyd was always calling on a bottom—like a lover—to come up and be touched.

"So you haf tudge boddom?" Lehmann had asked, the day that Boyd had gone over to see him, and beamed on him with his remote, early-man smile. Then he had added, "Wich boddom?"

"The bottom of the bottom," Boyd had replied. It had seemed so at the time. Lehmann had gazed at him sadly, stroking the lobes of his ears.

"Mister Boyt," he had said, "woot you like to meed a boddom?"

"A which?" Boyd had replied, not sure that he had caught it.

"A man who hass tudge boddom," Lehmann had answered, and left the room. Boyd had thought the idea original with himself. He had sat there waiting—Lehmann had spoken to someone as an adult would speak to a child, then he returned with Paula Kahler and her knitting, her luminous gaze. No comment had been necessary. She had stood before them, smiling in her usual trance of blessedness.

"Mister Boyt—" Lehmann had said, "the boddom of the boddom iss a lonk way down."

"Facts are stranger than fiction," Boyd had replied.

"*Fax?*" the old man had cried, "*wot* fax? If you haf tudge boddom there are no fax. It iss all viction. Only viction iss a fack!"

Boyd had said nothing. Across his mind—as once he had felt the wing of madness—he felt the imprint of a fact, one blown to him directly from the horse's mouth. With it the knowledge that he might, one day, both touch bottom and push off from it.

"What's he want his *ears* for?" the boy asked.

Boyd leaned forward to see what ears, and saw them. The hero was there in the runway below them, holding, like flowers, the bull's two bloody ears.

"What do you want a coonskin hat for?" said Boyd, although a coonskin hat was a covering for the head, needed no explaining, and had nothing in common with a pair of bull's ears. The boy's gaze showed it.

"Now you're being silly," he said.

The words, the words and the music, by his grandmother. What would he think, this sensible lad, in his sensible frontier suit with sparkler pistols, of a man who had once torn the smelly pocket from a ballplayer's pants. Not his hat, nor his shoes, not even his ears. Just the pocket to his pants. What would this practical little monster think of that?

"You want to know how silly I am?" Boyd asked.

He did. Very much so.

"Whose ears you got?" he probed. "A rabbit's?"

"I don't have any ears," said Boyd, "nor even hats. What I've got is a dirty, smelly pocket."

"Where?" said the boy.

"Not here with me," Boyd replied, and slapped his raincoat pockets. "I've got it at home. It's a big, stinky flannel pocket."

Did he believe that? He took a suck on his gun barrel, reflected, then said, "You don't have the pants to go with it?"

Boyd shook his head. "No, no pants," he said. He thought about that himself, then added, "Instead of cutting off his ears, what I did was snatch the pocket of his pants."

"Why was it stinky?" said the boy.

"This man was a baseball player," said Boyd, "and his pants got stinky in hot summer weather. When he slid into base he slid in on the seat of his pants." That impressed him. "His name was Tyrus Raymond Cobb," Boyd continued, "but they called him the Georgia Peach because he was so good."

He followed that. He glanced up quickly to see if Boyd was pulling his leg. "How'd you get it?" he asked.

"Oh—" said Boyd, shrugging, "I just tore it off." They watched the bull. He was as big as Ty, but he didn't run the bases at all as gracefully. Ty could pivot. He had had to, at least, that once. "You like to hear—" Boyd said, "how I snatched Ty Cobb's pocket?"

Up and down, like the handle of a pump, the boy wagged his head.

"Well—" Boyd said, feeling his way, "it's quite a little story. He was playing for the Tigers, I was going to Farnam School at the time. He came out to play in Omaha, that fall, on a barnstorming tour."

"Omaha has the stockyards," said the boy.

"That's right," said Boyd. "Used to smell them all summer. Noticed the smell was still there on our way down here. But the old school—" he paused there a moment, "the old school was gone."

"The one where you went?"

"On the corner of 29th and Farnam," said Boyd. "Gone now. Big used-car lot in its place. School was one of those square, red brick buildings with a brick walk around it, yard covered with cinders. We played pom-pom-pullaway during recess, and before school.

On one side of the yard we had these trees we swung around until we wore the bark off them. All the first floor windows usually had pictures on them, paper pumpkins, Santa Clauses, witches riding on brooms. One of the second floor windows had this landing on the fire escape."

He stopped there, glanced to see how the boy was taking it.

"We got a chute," said the boy. "We got a shoot-the-chute," and made a noise with his lips to indicate the way they shot it.

"We didn't—" Boyd continued, "we had this fire escape. To get out on it you crawled through the window. One of the jobs I had was to crawl through the window twice a day."

"What for?"

"My job was to clean the erasers. The place to clean them was out on the fire escape. I'd go out with the erasers and slap them on the bricks till they were clean. All around the window, where I slapped them, the red bricks were almost white with the chalk dust. So were my hands. Then I'd get it on my pants trying to rub them clean." He paused, but the boy sat listening. "Inside the room we had these desks, facing the blackboard, and over near the door a walnut Victrola. Another thing I did was to wind the Victrola. I played the Victrola every morning, when we did exercises to the Clock Store record, the volume turned up high but the clocks turned down a little slow. When the motor ran down I would stop exercising and go wind it up."

"Were you the teacher's pet?"

"I guess I was. When we all pledged the flag I was the one who held it. When anything important happened, I read it out loud from the Current Events."

They faced the ring, the huge bull-ox with his horns hooked in the mattress on the side of the horse, the rider out of the saddle, poised like a mosquito with his spear shaft into the bull's hump, but all three without movement, as if waiting for the shutter to snap.

"And now it's gone?" asked the boy.

"Gone—" Boyd replied, and spread out his hands, as if it had all disappeared at that moment. "The real thing never lasts, you know," he added, before he realized what he had said. Was that true? Strangely enough, it seemed to be. It was the unreal thing that lasted, the red-brick phantasm in Boyd's mind, complete with fire escape, erasers, and the listening dog in the Victrola horn. "Where was I?" said Boyd, wanting confirmation.

"Pledging the flag," said the boy.

"Oh, yes—" said Boyd. "Well, let's get out to the ball park—it was over near the stockyards—where we had seats right along the rail, the way we do here. A lot of other people were behind the chicken wire, where they wouldn't get hit. They'd all come out to watch Cobb play, and maybe hit a home run."

"Did he hit one?"

"He did—and he didn't," Boyd replied. "Due to what happened, it's pretty hard to say. He hit it, that is, but he never got as far as home with it."

The boy moved in closer. He let the gun he was holding rest on Boyd's knee.

"Reason he didn't—" Boyd went on, clearing his throat, "was that when he rounded third, they headed him off. I mean, I did. It just so happened that it happened to be me."

Was it possible? Boyd sometimes wondered himself. He did once more, then said, "Your granddaddy was there and saw it. You can ask him." The boy wheeled around in the seat to ask him, but McKee was not there. "If what you want is proof," Boyd said, "I guess the proof is in the pocket." Before the question was asked he continued, "You probably wonder, why his pocket? Why not something useful like his hat, say—?"

He stopped there. The proof was not in the pocket. Had it ever been? The proof from now on was in the telling.

"It's quite a story, son—" he said, and watched the big bull, the darts waving in his hump, go along the fence looking for what no bullring offered. A corner. There was no place to hide. Trailing him, like Mack Sennett detectives, were the matador and his assistants. Impersonal as fate. Goya-like harpies in the fading light. "—Although I don't remember the start of the game. Somewhere about the middle he hit this foul ball—Ty Cobb did, that is—and I got my hands on it. A little later he hit what should have been a home run. The fielders lost track of the ball and stood around the flagpole out in center, and I don't really know if it ever came down or not. While it was still up there, somewhere, I went over the fence. I had this foul ball that he'd hit, and I wanted it autographed. I crossed the foul line between first base and home plate, and by the time Ty was rounding third, I was on the line with this ball in my hand. I had him blocked off. It just might be he thought the ball I had was the one he had hit. We'll never know. All I know is that he came around third base, saw me with the ball, and headed for the dugout. Turns out he also saw, coming up behind me, about five hundred kids who had the same idea, half of them with new balls they had bought and wanted autographed. As I say, he headed for the dugout, but before he made it we had closed in on him. Coming up behind him, I got my hands on his pants. On his pocket, that is. When he kept on going, the pocket came off. I didn't notice till later— quite a bit later, since they had to call the game off—that I'd dropped the ball I went out to get autographed. So all I had was his pocket. Piece of flannel with grass stains on one corner of it. I put my name on one side of it, and used it to kneel on when I played marbles. So long as I stuck to marbles, I guess it brought me luck."

"Why didn't you just stick to marbles?" asked the boy, and in his eyes, the ice-blue eyes of the Scanlons, Boyd saw a child's pity for the man who had turned to squirting pop. He had no answer. If he had stuck to marbles, would he have been *champeen*? Would he have slain the wild bull, walked on the water, and carried off the girl with the ice-blue eyes to live happily ever after, eating candied apples and divinity fudge? He would never know. Like that home run the Georgia Peach had hit, the ball would never come down. It would remain, forever suspended, high in the cloudland out in center, where the fielders, with their eyes on the heavens, circled the flagpole.

Firmly, feeling the round head beneath it, he placed his hand on the coonskin hat, and let it slide back to where he could grip the coonskin by the tail. Gently, as if it might be alive, he raised it from the boy's head, then said—

"Your Uncle Gordon will now bring a dead coon back to life."

The boy did not grab for it, nor cry out, but watched his Uncle Gordon, as though that hat was a lasso, twirl it by the tail above his head, faster and faster, then let it fly. They both watched it, a headless bird with a long fur tail, and strange plumage, soar out over the ring, lift a moment on the draft, then drop to the sand. The bullfighter did not see it, nor did his *peones*, since they stood as if in mourning, watching the bull die, and the roar from the crowd they took as a sign of a deed well done.

"Go get it, kid—" said Boyd, softly, and took him by the arms, held him over the rail, then let him drop on the sand in the runway. He reappeared, like a spring-wind toy in the costume of a frontier doll, through the slit in the funk hole and scooted like a BB across the ring. A troop of small fry, all of them authentic Indians, who had come in with the mules when the gates had opened, also headed for the coonskin, but Davy Crockett got there first. He had recovered his hat, but in the process lost his senses. He ran around wildly, pursued by Indians, wheeling to shoot one dead, scalp another, then ride off in all directions firing volleys of sparks into the air. Some little Indians watched him, others straddled the bull while his body was still warm and the mules had him moving, or they hung like water skiers to his frazzled tail. High on the slopes of the bullring, burning like flares, sheets of flaming newspaper soared skyward, suddenly cooled, powdered, and fell like a rain of ash.

"The bool iss det!" he heard Lehmann croak, "lonk lif the bool!" and they had come to the end—or was it the beginning—of the rites of spring? On the cooling sand the coonskin hat trailed showers of sparks.

"Touch bottom," Boyd said, softly, and feeling it beneath him, he inhaled, pushed off.

Someone behind him shouted *Sit down*.

McKee McKee sat down. That still left people standing, but the voice had shouted in English, and McKee had the feeling it was meant for him. He wasn't where he belonged at all, but since the seat was empty he sat down in it. Just in time. Right down there below him the bull came in. The sand seemed to glow like the paint on a road sign, but McKee couldn't tell you what color the bull was. His horns looked white, like they'd been painted, and he wondered if it worked out like night baseball, nothing much showing but the diamond, the ball and the bat. Problem for the bull was to figure what the pitcher had on the ball.

What McKee couldn't figure was why the bull, after fanning the air for five or ten minutes, didn't catch on sooner there was nothing behind that fool red cloth. The man stood there just like a post, but the bull went for the cloth. What tricked him? Or were bulls just naturally that dumb? By the time he began to wise up a little, it was too late. They had a rule that wouldn't let him come back for another chance.

What did Boyd say?

Before you pity the bull, McKee, don't forget he's had a chance you haven't.

That's okay by me, McKee had said. Before he thought about it. After thinking he wondered what the devil it meant. Did he mean to say McKee had wanted to gore someone? But who the devil ever knew

210

just what it was Boyd meant. Including Boyd. He was a great one to bamboozle himself.

Take that fool pocket. If you asked Boyd he would tell you something fancy as to why it was he hung on to it—if you asked McKee it was just a fancy way of covering up. Covering up what? The fact that he'd dropped the ball. It took a sharp sort of person to hear him tell it and keep track of that.

Another instance, one McKee had forgotten, were those so-called letters he got from his mother, which weren't really letters at all since she could mail them second-class. She just turned the flap in, she didn't seal it, or care if people read what was inside or not, since they were just clippings she had snipped from the local paper. The line Boyd took, when McKee discovered that, was that his mother was smarter than Uncle Sam, and saved all sorts of money by writing to him second-class. The way he told it you could overlook the fact that his mother never sent him any real letters. Just these clippings he could have read in the paper himself.

The ones McKee had seen were all about the Cretes, Ashley Crete in particular, since he was nearly always off somewhere, doing something interesting. Mrs. Boyd would underline in ink the important points. McKee got the feeling that the printed word meant a lot to her. She could write a letter, if she had to, but it was usually just a line or two from some clipping she didn't want to send because she thought it might get lost. But they were letters, in a way, since Gordon only read the underlined parts. It gave him the kernel of what she had to say. It kept him on his toes, since every time Ashley won anything, or went anywhere, Boyd would get a letter by second-class mail.

Mrs. Boyd had the kind of horse sense Boyd could have used, but hadn't been born with, since she never lost sight of the forest for the trees. When McKee had come back from Omaha he had gone over to tell her about the ball game, and how Boyd had snatched the pocket from the ballplayer's pants. McKee had sat on the porch, which was so close to the ground grass grew through the cracks in it, and Mrs. Boyd had sat in her rocker and rocked. She was a white-haired woman, more like a grandmother, and McKee had felt silly talking about baseball, but when he had finished she said—

"Did Gordon drop that ball?"

McKee had lost track of that ball himself. After all that had happened it hardly seemed important that he'd dropped the ball. But his mother had seen right through it, which was why, in McKee's opinion, Boyd left home so early and never got along too well with her. You couldn't pull the wool over the eyes of a woman like that.

Nor any other woman, for that matter, which was maybe why Boyd was ending up alone with just some stockings on his doorknob, and that fool pocket in his grip. Boyd had pointed out himself, when they saw him in New York, that the pocket was the only thing he'd ever kept hold of—but even that was just a way of making you forget he'd dropped all the balls. Right up till his dying day he would probably keep it handy, or wave it at you, the way the bullfighter played around with that cloth. Pulling the wool over the bull's eyes with it, or using it to cover up, when you got him cornered, the wild streak in his nature that had ruined him. He was every bit as stubborn, if you asked McKee, as old man Scanlon. He just refused to believe what he didn't want to believe.

What did it lead to?

McKee had just read about it somewhere. Stubborn old man you couldn't tell anything. Mad as a coot. McKee had thought of Boyd all the time he sat reading it. This old fool had the Bible Flood on the brain, so that when he saw water that was all he could think of. Next thing you know, he would try to walk on it.

Out in the West somewhere, in Utah or Nevada, they put in this big dam to hold up the water, and in time it backed up and covered the town where this old man lived. He'd been out of town at the time, prospecting somewhere. When he'd come out of the mountains and seen what had happened he thought it was the Flood. The water had backed up, just the way it was supposed to, clean up the valley to where he'd been living, and the town was said to be forty feet under water at the time. Everybody in the town knew what was going to happen but this old man. When he came out of the mountains he saw this lake where the desert had been. Right where he had his shack, since the water was rising, just the top of his windmill was sticking out, the wheel still spinning, as he said, like a big water bug. Something about it made quite an impression on him. Did on McKee too, the way the old man told it, like he was Noah up there on the mountain, with the whole world flooded instead of just that desert valley of his. Quite a bit the way, if McKee understood it, the Biblical fathers got the same idea when the Nile, or whatever river it was, flooded the place. They thought the world was flooded, since that was how it looked to them. It looked about the same, or even worse, to that old man. He didn't have the Lord to fall back on, the way Noah did. He didn't have any animals to save, or any trees to build him an ark. And while he stood there looking, the top of that windmill was covered up.

The article didn't go on to say if he had grasped the facts of the case or not, but McKee would say he hadn't. The facts wouldn't have meant a thing to him. The engineers could talk till they were blue in the face about the dam down below, backing up the water, but what the old man saw from the mountain would always be the Flood. There were people like that. His wife's father was one of them. If he saw a bunch of cows with horns he would swear they were buffalo. If they ever backed water up around Lone Tree he probably just wouldn't believe it, since he hadn't read the Bible, and he'd drown any day rather than admit to anything he didn't believe. Boyd was every bit as crazy, but in a different way. He'd believe in almost anything, if it was just unlikely enough. Other people standing up, McKee stood up. What had he missed? The big bull, with these boys around him, was there along the fence. The one with the sword spread his cloth on the sand like he expected the bull to walk on it. The bull put his head down, as if to sniff it, and then the one with the sword, as if he meant to club him, leaned away over and poked him with it at the back of his head. Just that little poke did it. He dropped all in a heap, and the band began to play.

The man below McKee turned around at that point and looked up the aisle, like he expected somebody, and in his eyes, as in farmhouse windows, McKee could see the reflection of something burning. He turned to look at the bonfire, a good-sized one, high up in the ring. Kids old enough to know better were throwing on it anything that would burn. That explained why it was they made the ring out of concrete, with the seats that would freeze you, since anything that was soft, or made of wood, they would burn to the ground. He watched the fire, the way the sparks shot upward, and remembered the time when he and Boyd —it had been mostly Boyd—had burned the Kaiser Devil in effigy. They made him out of a scarecrow, with a big tin funnel for a hat. Any bonfire at all, with kids running around it, made McKee think of that.

When he looked back at the bullring it was swarming with kids. Maybe thirty of them, the way they'd swarm out on a diamond after a ball game, hooting like Indians and raising hell generally. Made him think of Boyd, and that fool pocket, and against the sand, bright as it was, he could see four or five of the little rascals astraddle the bull. The one they didn't have room for rode out in back, hanging on to his tail. That was just about the wildest sort of thing McKee had ever seen. The body of that bull still warm, more than likely, and those kids straddling it.

The ring was full of them, all shapes and sizes, but one little tyke struck McKee as familiar. He ran around wild, like they all did, but he never stopped shooting off sparks. It was so dark in the ring that the sparks made it easy to keep track of him. He was like a bug, the way he scooted, and McKee had to wait till he got a little closer, right there below him, before he saw the tail on the coonskin hat.

"Gordon!" he yelled, so loud he almost lost his voice. When he yelled again he could hardly hear it above the band. The boy heard nothing. Off he scooted trailing a shower of sparks. Just yelling like that made McKee dizzy, he dropped down in the seat, but he no sooner felt the cold than he thought of Mrs. McKee, popped up.

But he didn't holler. Bygod—he said to himself—let Boyd get him. If something happened to that boy, let Boyd explain it. He went around the curving aisle, not even running—let Boyd, this time, do the running—he was so dam crazy to climb over a fence, well, now he could climb. For the first time in his life there would be some excuse for his doing it. That wild streak in him. For the first time in his life it would be of some use.

McKee reached the aisle, but there was Boyd, if he could believe his eyes, down there smiling at him. Was he crazy?

"For Pete's sake, Gordon!" said McKee.

"What's the trouble?" he replied.

"If something should happen to that boy—" said McKee, but it left him speechless, just to think of it. "Gordon—" he said, waving his arm, "you get in there and get that boy."

"You know how kids are—" said Boyd, "when they see a fence."

"I know how that boy is," said McKee, "and I know who it was that put him over. I'm going to ask you to go in and get him, and to do it quick."

Boyd stopped smiling. McKee didn't like the look on his face.

"If he was your boy—" said McKee, "you could do as you like. Could if he was mine. But this boy—"

"If—?" said Boyd.

It crossed McKee's mind that he was really crazy. The wild streak had got the best of him.

"If this boy's name is Gordon—" said Boyd.

"This is no time for horseplay," said McKee, and cupped his hands to his mouth, shouted, "Oh, Gordon!"

"If you want him to come," said Boyd, "you've got to call him by his name."

If McKee had had the strength he would have turned and run. He didn't want to hear. "Boyd—" he said, to shut him up, "if you don't get that boy—" and Boyd turned to face the ring, cupped his hands to his face, and like the clown he was sang out the Davy Crockett business.

> "Davy, Da-vy, Da-vyyyy Crockett
> King of the Wild Frontier!"

McKee saw the boy wheel around as if someone had grabbed his arm. He raised his gun and fired some sparks at Boyd, shouted "You're dead!"

"Come over here, Davy Crockett!" Boyd said.

The boy just stood there with the gun in his hand. He was not going to come, and McKee could see it —he had as stubborn a streak in him as Boyd—but he slipped that gun back into the holster, and came. He just walked, he didn't run, he just walked clean across the ring to the funk hole, slipped in through it, then came along the alley to where Boyd stood.

"Am I Davy Crockett now?" he said.

"Sure you are," said Boyd, "you're the old frontiersman," and leaned over the rail at the front and got hold of him. He pulled him up and stood him in the seat, brushed the sand off his front. "Here's your man," Boyd said, slapped him across the bottom, but the boy just stood there.

"I got his hat now, too," said the boy.

"Sure you have," said Boyd, "go show it to your grandma—" and set him down in the aisle, gave him a shove.

"Son," said McKee, trying an old tack, "you want to bring your great-granddaddy along with you?"

Putting the boy in charge of something, especially the old man, usually brought him to heel. But this time it didn't. The old man popped up, like he'd heard that, and went along the rail by himself. It wasn't like him to move a foot without the boy, and McKee wondered if that was more of Boyd's doing.

"Now you come here—" he said, raising his voice, but the boy just stood there, doing nothing. McKee needed help, that is he could use it, but where could he turn with his wife gone and just this foreigner with his mental patient there in their seats? In spite of all the racket the woman, Mrs. Kahler, looked like she was asleep. Her head lolled on his shoulder, and he didn't look too wide awake himself.

"Gordon," said McKee, "you come *here*—" but the boy neither moved nor sassed him back. McKee would have liked it better if he'd hollered *no*, or fired off his gun.

"You better go along, kid," Boyd said, and as you might expect, he came right along. McKee gave his hand a shake when he got a grip on it, but the boy didn't seem to notice that, or fight it. McKee could feel the ring sand on it that stuck to his own sweaty palm. It made him feel a little silly, since nothing much had happened. Nothing at all.

"His grandmother thinks a lot of this boy," he said aloud, to help explain how he had acted, and nine times out of ten the boy would have said how much *he* thought of his grandmother. But this time he didn't. It wasn't like him. McKee wondered if running around like that hadn't made him pretty tired.

"I guess I better get this boy where he belongs," he said, meaning in bed. Even the boy understood it.

"And where is that?" said Boyd.

Did McKee see him smile? Just the top of his head was lighted—the way it had been in that New York attic—the light in such a way that McKee couldn't see his face. Something about it, the way McKee felt about it, was the same. That anything might happen. The way Mrs. McKee had felt about Boyd most of her life. McKee too, but he usually didn't seem to mind. But the way he felt about it now troubled him. The swarm of kids on the sand, the bonfires high in the bullring, and the way Boyd just stood there, smiling at him, gave McKee the eerie feeling he had in Texas when they butchered that hog. What had it been? That there was more going on than met the eye. More to the shooting of the hog, the clotted pail of flies, the shaved body of the hog like a corpse in the moonlight, with the head gazing at him, through its third eye, from the pail. Didn't he see on Boyd, as on the face of that hog, the same amused smile?

"You know as well as I do, Boyd—" he began, but

he could sense the trouble coming. That wild streak in him. He took a fresh grip on the boy's hand and said, "This boy belongs to his grandma."

"You're too late," Boyd replied. Did McKee see him shrug?

"Too late for *what?*" said McKee. Not that he wanted to know, God knows, but he just stood there. How did Mrs. McKee always put it? That Boyd had them bewitched.

"The kid's changed," said Boyd, as if the kid wasn't there. As if this change struck him as a sad one. "He's got a new pitch. He's just torn the pocket off Ty Cobb's pants."

"Don't you go putting ideas into this boy's head," said McKee, and gave the boy's hand a tug.

"You're too late," replied Boyd. "Whose boy you think he is?"

"You watch what you're saying, Boyd," said McKee, and dragged the boy up the aisle to get him out of earshot.

"Right now," Boyd yelled, "he's the son of Davy Crockett. But any day now he may swap it for a pocket!"

"When he does!—" McKee hollered, shouting like an old fool, "I hope it doesn't do to him what it did to you!"

Then he wheeled and almost ran along the aisle, dragging the boy. Near the exit he suddenly remembered, looked around wildly, and said, "You see your great-granddaddy?"

They didn't. When the old man wanted to he could scoot off at quite a clip. He couldn't see, but he could smell his way around like a dog.

"We got to find your great-granddaddy, son," he said, since he knew they would never be lucky enough to lose him. If they did, somebody from Omaha or Lincoln would run into him. There would be another article to the effect that his children had taken him clean down to Mexico and ditched him.

"You got better eyes than your grandpa," he said. "You look for him."

He wiped the palm of his own sweaty hand on his pants, then wiped the boy's hand with a piece of wadded Kleenex. The boy let him do it. It wasn't like him to stand there and not complain.

"I'll bet you're hungry as a wolf, aren't you?" said McKee.

The boy did not reply. Usually he was full of talk and tugging on McKee like a dog on a leash. Now he just stood there like a little man. Was he shivering? There were more of those bonfires high in the ring, and McKee could see, now, why they had lit them. It was crisp. It got pretty cold when the sun went down.

"It's a wonder those kids don't burn the place down," he said, but the boy didn't bite at it. He didn't fire off his gun. Maybe he had caught a bug, or something. He stood there with his mouth hanging open, like he had adenoids.

"Son—" said McKee, "I tell you what we do. What do you say me and you have a little secret?" Was he listening? McKee gave his hand a tug. "Suppose just you and me know you were down in the bullring, nobody else?"

"Uncle Gordon," said the boy.

"All right, him too. But just me, you and Uncle Gordon. Not grandma. Not great-granddaddy. Just him, me and you."

Did the boy follow that? No answer.

"It would just make your grandma nervous," said McKee, "and she wouldn't let us go to any more bullfights."

"Ty Cobb too," said the boy.

"*Who?*" said McKee. He just blurted it out, then

to cover up he said, "All right, *him* too. But let's not say where you saw him. Let's not say—" His mouth a little dry, McKee paused to moisten his lips. It wasn't only women who could have intuitions. Did women know that? He had had one, a good one, years ago when he had known that Boyd would never have his own family, and now he had another. A good intuition, but a bad effect. He knew better than the boy knew it himself, what was on his mind. He knew it was a pocket, he knew all about it since McKee had seen it, and the boy hadn't, but he had to keep the boy from so much as mentioning it. If he could do that he might not even know that he had it on his mind—not as well as McKee did—and it might pass off like most of the things on a boy's mind.

"Let grandpa buy you something," said McKee, "what do you want grandpa to buy you?" and led him into the tunnel, where it was getting dark. Up ahead there was light, a little of it, and making the turn on the ramp McKee could see the lean forked legs of the old man. Almost trotting. Doing his damdest to get himself lost. Bygod, let him, thought McKee. Just let him. If that's what he wanted, why, let him. So he stopped right there, in the tunnel, took out that cigar he hadn't finished, and took all the time in the world lighting it up. He gave the boy the band on it, for his collection, and slipped it down on his trigger finger.

"There you are," he said. "Now how you like that?"

He didn't say anything.

"Let's take it a little easy now," he said, "your grandma might wonder why you got so sweaty."

Running around in the ring like a yahoo had got him worked up. As often as McKee wiped his hand off, it got sticky again. They went easy up the ramp, letting people go by them, giving the old fool time enough to lose himself forever, if that's what he had in mind. Right outside the gate a man was selling bulls, little black paper bulls with white horns on them.

"You can have a bull," said McKee to the boy. "You want a bull?"

"It's not a bull if you buy it," said the boy.

Who told him that? No need for McKee to guess. He was fond of the boy, but he had a strong impulse to take the paper bull and crown him with it.

"Okay—" said McKee, "since you're so smart I'll just buy a little bull for myself. And while I'm at it I think I'll buy myself a pair of these real horns."

Which he did. Just as if he was out of his mind. One of those fool toy bulls, and mounted on a big board, a pair of real bull horns. Two hundred pesos. That was almost twenty dollars for a pair of dam horns. He had to carry the bull, since it seemed a little fragile, and to take the horns he had to drop the boy's hand. Off he scooted.

"Now you come back here!" called McKee.

But of course he didn't. He ran like he was crazy, but he seemed to know where he was going. Right down the road to their own station wagon, where the lights were on. McKee saw the door open, then he saw his grandma hug him like she already knew all about it, even before he told her, but she could hardly wait to hear it again. 'Way at the back of the car, since the lights were on, he could see old Scanlon sitting up spruce as a fiddle, proud of the fact that he'd ducked McKee and made it back by himself. Very likely he had told her that McKee had walked off and left him somewhere. The way he did in Laredo. Scooting back across the bridge like McKee was trying to kidnap him.

McKee walked up slow, but when he reached the door nobody seemed to care, or open it for him. They let him stand there with this bull, with these horns he was holding, while they sat smug inside, like they were in a phone booth, and he would have to wait until they had put through their call. All the windows were up, and only the button on the dashboard would run them down. But he could hear the boy yelling like his heart was broke. McKee could tell you, even though he couldn't hear it, just what it was that boy was yelling, and that it wasn't for a bull, a bull's horns, or anything like that. Not any longer. No, he was yelling for something else. He was yelling for something, McKee could tell you, that he couldn't buy even if he had the money, and gazing at McKee were the serene blue eyes of his wife. Ice-blue, Boyd called them. In matters like that he usually proved to be right.

Other SIGNET Books
by Outstanding American Writers

SANCTUARY AND REQUIEM FOR A NUN
by William Faulkner

Two violent novels of Temple Drake, a young girl in the clutch of a macabre murderer. (#T1900—75¢)

BAND OF ANGELS **by Robert Penn Warren**

The powerful and romantic story of a Kentucky belle who was sold into slavery. (#T1872—75¢)

APPOINTMENT IN SAMARRA **by John O'Hara**

Three days in the life of a man destroyed by his inability to come to grips with his personality. (#CP177—60¢)

THE NAKED AND THE DEAD **by Norman Mailer**

The famous bestseller about the fighting men sent on an impossible mission in the Pacific. (#Q2460—95¢)

THE GROUP **by Mary McCarthy**

One of the most talked-about novels of recent years, this is the daring and brilliant story of eight Vassar graduates trying to cope with life and love during the turbulent depression years of the thirties. (#Q2501—95¢)

ANDERSONVILLE **by MacKinlay Kantor**

The Pulitzer prize winning novel of the infamous Civil War prison. (#Q2142—95¢)

LIE DOWN IN DARKNESS **by William Styron**

An outstanding novel about a tortured girl and the people and events that lead her to the brink of despair.
(#Q2655—95¢)